THE LITTLE BOOK OF
BREAKING 80

How to Shoot in the 70s (Almost) Every Time You Play Golf

By Shane Jones

Published by NJM Publishing

Table of Contents

Forward

Have you ever broken 80? If so, are you able to shoot scores in the 70s consistently? If you're like the majority of golfers, the answer is probably no.

In fact, according to a recent study conducted by the Golf Channel, despite all of the advances in golf equipment and ball technology, despite the availability of high-speed video cameras, despite the vast availability of information on the Internet, and despite the many golf instruction books and videos by the best players and instructors in the game, the average golf score for all golfers is right around 100. For men, the average is about 97. For woman, it is 114. Indeed, despite all of these advances, golfers as a whole have not improved significantly over the last half century. We all know that golf is a challenging game, but is it really so hard that the average golfer can barely break 100?

When it comes to breaking 80, according to the same study, the picture becomes even bleaker. Only about 6% of all men and 1% of women are able to break 80 consistently. Looking at these daunting numbers, it might be easy to conclude that the hope of breaking 80 on a consistent basis is a pipe dream at best for most golfers.

So what gives? Is golf really such a hopelessly impossible game? Should we just resign ourselves to the reality that most golfers are fated to spend their golfing lives stuck in mediocrity shooting scores in the 90s or even the 100s? Or might it be possible that there's simply something wrong with the way we learn to play this perplexing game that is keeping us from playing much better?

Over the years I've played with and observed dozens of golfers with the ability to break 80. These golfers include everyone from tour-caliber pros to 11-year-old kids to petite women, overweight and out-of-shape men and even retired grandfathers. I've also spent years analyzing my own game. In my own golfing lifetime, which has now spanned three decades, there have been stretches of time when I have been able to break 80 consistently, while at other times I have not, and my progress has been anything but linear.

In observing these 70s shooters and in analyzing my own game, I began to notice some interesting trends. Most 70s shooters I played with (including myself) did not hit the ball particularly long. Many weren't particularly good drivers of the ball at all (me again). Others missed far more greens than they hit (that's me too). None of these golfers were prodigiously athletic or even particularly coordinated (yep). And yet all these golfers, in all of their shapes and sizes, ages and backgrounds, displayed the ability to break 80, time and time again. What is it that makes these golfers, who on the surface do not appear physically any different from less accomplished golfers, able to break 80 while most other golfers cannot even come close to doing so?

Having studied these accomplished golfers along with analyzing my own game over many years, I began to notice some common traits shared by all accomplished golfers that are noticeably different from those shared by struggling golfers. Once I synthesized these common traits, through a lifetime of trial and error I finally stumbled upon what I believe to be the "magic formula" for breaking 80 consistently. What I found was quite shocking, and flies in the face of much of what conventional golf wisdom preaches.

Having discovered this "magic formula," or blueprint if you will, I have been pleased to discover that provided I simply follow this blueprint, I'm now able to break 80 on a consistent basis despite my limited natural talent and limited time to play and practice, whereas before, my progress was haphazard and short-lived at best despite investing a tremendous amount of time and energy, not to mention money, in a futile attempt to improve.

Furthermore, I have found this blueprint to be unfailing in its effectiveness. As long as I adhere to its principles and focus on the "right things" instead of the "wrong things" (I'll discuss what these "right things" and "wrong things" are later on in the book), the formula is almost magical in its predictability and consistency in enabling me to break 80 more times than not, or at least have a very good opportunity to do so even on days when my game is a little off.

So what is this "magic formula" that enables me and these other rare golfers to break 80 on a consistent basis while the rest of the golfing population continues to spin on the endless merry-go-round of failure and frustration? After years of study and analysis and trial and error, I've concluded that the secret to breaking 80 lies not in natural talent, athleticism, or even swing technique.

Rather, the ability to break 80 has to do with a very precise approach to the game and the development of a very specific set of golf skills which, whether through ignorance or industry conspiracy, are either unknown or simply ignored by most players and teachers alike. One of the sad facts about golf is that only a fortunate few golfers ever discover and dedicate themselves to mastering the true scoring skills that lead unfailingly to shooting low scores, while the rest of the golfing population struggles and suffers endlessly with mediocrity and frustration.

The purpose of this book, therefore, is to lift the veil of confusion and finally reveal the True Keys to Breaking 80. My goal is to empower frustrated golfers and arm you, the reader, with the true knowledge you need to finally begin to surely and steadily improve your scores, with an approach based on sound principles that any golfer can easily learn and apply, to the point where provided you follow these principles faithfully, you will eventually gain the ability to break 80, not just as a one-time fluke, but over and over again.

As you read the Little Book of Breaking 80, I believe you'll find that the "magic formula" for breaking 80 is well within your grasp, and that if you will only apply the principles that you will learn in this book, your scores will begin to improve dramatically, to the point where breaking 80 will no longer be a distant pipe dream, but a distinct reality well within your reach.

This book is divided into two parts. In Part One, I begin by exposing and discussing many of the myths and misconceptions most golfers have about the game of golf, as well as what I believe to be flaws with the general approach to teaching, learning, practicing and improving at the game. These myths, misconceptions and flaws form the basis for a belief system and approach to the game that makes it all but impossible for most golfers to maximize their ability to shoot lower scores, much less break 80 on a consistent basis. In order for you to realize your true potential as a golfer, it is essential that you first recognize and then ultimately break free of this flawed and limiting belief system and approach to the game.

In Part Two, I specifically reveal what I believe to be the True Keys to Breaking 80, including precisely what the task of breaking 80 involves, those aspects of the game you will most need to focus on improving in order to lower your scores, and the specific approach you will need to adopt in order to maximize your scoring ability and gain the ability to break 80, not just as an occasional fluke, but time and time again as a reflection of your true newfound ability.

Introduction: My Own Breaking 80 Journey

My inspiration for writing this book came when I realized that my own golfing progression was a microcosm for the struggles and frustrations that I see every day in other devoted golf enthusiasts. If you don't care to read about my background as a golfer, feel free to skip this brief section, but I include it to illustrate my struggles and failures to improve my golf game through the conventional approaches preached by the industry, as well as to show what did work and why. Plus, you may identify some of your own golf struggles in the story of my own, which I think will resonate as we delve further into the book.

I'm not an accomplished professional golfer or even a teaching pro, but rather, an amateur golf enthusiast like you who spent the better part of 30 years struggling with this game before finally discovering the truth about what it takes to gain a measure of success in golf.

I was first introduced to the game of golf at the age of 12, when my best friend's father took the two of us out one day to the local 9-hole executive course and I got my first taste of this tantalizing game. I don't remember much about that round other than making two pars in a row through sheer beginner's luck, but from that day forward I was completely and utterly hooked. Little did I know then how much this game would become a part of me, and how many ups and downs and peaks and valleys and frustrations and struggles I would experience through golf along the way.

My golf career began with promise. By my second summer playing, I was shooting in the mid-80s and occasionally low-80s. I never practiced or "worked on my swing" and almost never hit balls on the range. I simply played rounds and engaged in friendly putting contests with my golf buddy.

In my second year I began to play a few junior tournaments. My results were mixed and nothing special, but I can remember shooting 81 and finishing in the top 10 in one of my first events, and also qualifying for the sectionals of the World Junior Golf Championship, where I had a great chance to earn a trip to San Diego for the finals until a lost ball and subsequent 9 on the back side cost me that opportunity.

Although I had made considerable progress in my first two years playing, the more I played the more eager I became to improve. I must confess though that although I had a burning desire to improve, I didn't really have much of a work ethic at that time. Instead, I sought out shortcuts to improvement by devouring golf instruction books in the local library, along with the many instruction articles in the issues of Golf Digest that I received by mail each month.

I believed that simply through reading and studying golf books and magazines I would discover the secret of the magical swing that would enable me to become a scratch golfer and, one day, a tour pro—my one and only childhood dream. However, something unexpected happened. The more I tried to implement the swing theories I read about, the worse I became. My once natural, flowing, thought-free swing became a tangled jumble of confused thoughts and jerky motions, resulting in an unnatural, mechanical nightmare of a golf swing.

I had been looking forward to playing golf on my high school team, but my high school golf career turned into a complete disaster. At the age of 15 I was consistently shooting in the low 80s, but by my senior year, I could barely break 90. Along the way I did manage to play a few random rounds in the high 70s, but by the time my high school golf career had ended, I was clearly a much worse player than when I began. The more I tried to fix my game, the worse I became. By the time I graduated high school, I realized that my dream of becoming a pro golfer was not going to be realized, but by then I didn't really care. I was frustrated with the game and frankly, sick of playing. Once high school ended I quit playing, got on with my life, and never gave golf a second thought.

Or so I thought. Fast forward about 10 years. By this time I was in graduate school, having worked for a few years before returning to college. I had forgotten about golf completely, but I was enjoying life, having worked a number of odd jobs before helping out for a few years in my family's business and, finally, working hard and succeeding in school. Although I was no longer playing golf, I was now an avid runner and swimmer, and had completed a marathon as well as a few triathlons.

Then it happened. I'm not even sure how it came about, but one day, while in college, the golf bug bit me out of nowhere, and suddenly I developed an urge to play again. I couldn't shake the nagging sense that I hadn't lived up to my potential as a teenager, and I wanted to give golf another shot. By then, I had developed a strong work ethic, and believed that this time, with a willingness to practice and work hard at the game, there was no way I could fail.

Although I was very busy with my studies and part-time job, I made room for golf. I would wake up at 4:30 a.m. to work out before classes, and in the early evening, after work and school, I would go to the local driving range and hit balls and practice chipping and putting. I didn't actually play that much, because I had decided to first commit to refining my skills. This time, I wasn't going to make the same mistakes I had made as a teenager. I would work diligently at my game and practice hard. Since I had become so confused by instruction as a youngster, I vowed that I would avoid golf instruction altogether and instead just use the flight of my ball and results on the range to tell me whether or not I was on the right track. Like Ben Hogan, my plan was to dig my game out of the dirt by sheer hard work and dedication!

I began to make some progress, but then a wrench got thrown into my plans when my life took an unexpected turn with an opportunity to go study and then work abroad in Japan for a few years. As you may know, it is both inconvenient and extremely expensive to play or practice golf in Japan. As a result, golf got sidetracked again as I focused on completing my studies and beginning my career.

However, even though I loved my life in Japan, the golf bug continued to gnaw at me. I still wanted to give myself a chance to realize my potential and see if I could become the type of golfer I had always dreamed of becoming. After about four years in Japan, at the age of 32 I decided to relocate back to Southern California in the U.S. in order to pursue my dream of becoming an accomplished golfer. Although I knew that becoming a competitive golfer was an extreme long shot, if not a downright pipe dream, I have always lived by the ethos of living life with no regrets and pursuing my dreams, however improbable they may be. I didn't want to look back when I was at the end of my life and wonder what might have been, and so I made the decision to move back to the U.S. in order to pursue my childhood dream.

Back in the U.S., I resumed the approach I had developed while at college. I worked out early in the morning and then after work, I would devote the rest of my day to working on my golf game. If dedication and hard work were the keys to improving at golf, then I had plenty of that to offer. I would hit anywhere from 100 to 300 balls per day in order to refine and groove my swing. I also worked diligently on my putting and short game.

I also played between one and three times per week, and indeed, in my first year back and focused on improving my golf game, I did improve considerably. I went from shooting around 95 at the outset to actually succeeding in breaking 80 a few times by the end of that first year. However, I still didn't feel like I was very good yet at any aspect of the game. I hit the ball fairly straight but I was an extremely short hitter and couldn't hit my long clubs very well at all. My short game still left a lot to be desired. And I wasn't a very good putter either, particularly on short putts. Plus, even though I had broken 80 a few times, I was still very inconsistent, and was just as likely to shoot 90 as break 80 for any given round.

So although I clearly had made some real progress by the end of my first year, I still felt like I was missing some essential component or piece of knowledge that would enable me to play great golf. One day, at the beginning of my second year working on my golf game, I was watching the Golf Channel and I saw something that I thought just might be the answer I was looking for.

This segment of the Golf Channel featured a golfer I had never heard of who was apparently the best ball striker who ever lived. His name was Moe Norman. I watched mesmerized as this golfer with a quirky swing and even quirkier personality hit ball after ball like a laser despite the fact that he was in his 70s. I thought to myself that surely this must be the answer to golf's Promised Land.

I therefore set about copying Moe Norman's swing in hopes of becoming as machine-like a ball striker as he. The results were disastrous. Not truly understanding what I was doing, my ball striking quickly went from mediocre to horrendous. I spent the better part of that year hooking nearly every shot off the planet in my attempt to copy the strong baseball-like grip and swing of Moe. As a result, I went from consistently shooting in the mid to low 80s and occasionally the 70s in year one to being barely able to break 100 in year two. Even after realizing that the Moe Norman swing was not going to work for me, the damage was already done and I had lost whatever semblance of a natural swing I originally had. I felt like a complete failure, as well as a total idiot for essentially making the same mistake I had made back when I was a teenager in attempting to fabricate a swing I read or heard about instead of nurturing and developing my own natural golf swing.

Ironically, the only thing that saved me from probably giving up the game completely was a mysterious back pain that I began to experience toward the end of year two. To this day I do not know what the source of this pain was. Perhaps it was the culmination of hitting too many balls and swinging in a physically unnatural manner, but the pain only manifest itself at impact when I attempted to strike a golf ball. I spent the first three months of my third year in golf attempting unsuccessfully to play through this pain, before realizing that I needed to seek medical help.

Over the next few months, I visited orthopedic specialists, chiropractors, acupuncturists, and massage therapists, but nothing I did would rid me of the sharp pain I experienced each time I attempted to hit a golf shot. I eventually realized that the only thing that was going to heal my back pain was a long, extended rest. Therefore, I made a decision to not even attempt to hit any more full shots for the rest of the year.

At this point, I felt like I had reached rock bottom in terms of my golf progress. I had begun my pursuit of golfing improvement full of enthusiasm and confidence, if not in my natural talent then at least in my dedication, work ethic, and desire to improve. And yet three years into my pursuit, not only was I playing just about as bad as I did when I first took up the game, I was now actually injured and couldn't even play golf at all.

Although I was deflated, quitting wasn't in my vocabulary, and so I did the only thing I could do: I dedicated myself to practicing my putting, which didn't hurt my back. Each day, while gazing wistfully over at the driving range envious of all of the able-bodied golfers able to work on their swings and hit full shots, I doggedly spent hours each week working on my putting.

Ever the tinkerer, I was inspired by Chris DiMarco's resurgence as a golfer thanks to adopting the claw grip, which was quite unique at the time, and began experimenting on my own until I came up with my own version of The Claw that involved clawing the left hand instead of the right.

This instantly transformed me into an almost machine-like putter, particularly from short range, and although I was frustrated that I wasn't able to actually play, this clear improvement in my putting refueled my desire to get back on the course.

After a couple months doing nothing but putting, I discovered that I could also practice my chipping and pitching without pain (although it still hurt when I attempted to hit bunker shots), and so I added short game work into my practice routine as well. I was happy to discover that as I focused intently on my chipping and pitching, I quickly improved my ability to hit the ball within close range to the hole from just off the green. It was in this manner that I concluded my third year in my pursuit of golfing glory.

By the beginning of my fourth year, I wanted to give taking a full swing another try, but I was also afraid of reinjuring myself. I compromised by going over to the nearby pitch and putt course and limiting myself to only taking partial full swings with my wedges. I was happy to discover that I could do this without any pain, and so my routine now consisted of working on my chipping and putting and playing rounds on the little pitch and putt course, where most of the holes were between 50 and 100 yards.

The effect of having worked exclusively on my short game was immediately noticeable, and simply by playing many rounds on the short course, my wedge game also began to improve dramatically. Within a couple months, I was shooting right around even par and occasionally under par on the short course. Although I realized that this wasn't the same as playing a full-length course, these positive results on the short course boosted my confidence, and I once again began to believe that just maybe I could became an accomplished player.

After about six months of exclusively playing on the short course and working on my short game, I decided to give full swings with longer clubs a try. The result was sort of a mixed bag. I still felt a small twinge of pain when I made a full swing, but it wasn't nearly as bad as it was before, and it didn't seem to get worse even after hitting a bucket of balls. However, I instinctively tried to avoid the sensation of pain, and as a result, my swing once again became altered as I attempted to find a way to swing that wasn't painful.

The result was that by the end of the year, two interesting developments occurred. Thanks to all of my short game practice, I was once again shooting decent scores. In fact, I was actually shooting better scores than ever before. I was breaking 80 quite regularly, about every one in three rounds, but this was due in no part to my swing, which in my attempt to swing free of pain, had developed some pretty significant flaws. My swing now had a massive over-the-top move, and in order to square my clubface from this over-the-top position, I also developed a grossly collapsed left wrist that made Dustin Johnson look like Freddie Couples at the top of the swing.

The result of this swing was that my stock shot with my driver and longer clubs was a massive slice. Only with my short irons and wedges was I able to hit the ball somewhat straight. Despite these major swing flaws, thanks to my short game and some prudent course management, borne out of necessity from hitting the ball all over the course, I evolved into the ultimate scrambler. In terms of skill level, I was probably about a 20 handicap ball striker with a scratch handicap short game. And yet I was shocked to discover that this combination regularly yielded scores in the 70s. In fact, that year I recorded my best 18-hole score to date, two 73s on a challenging course, as well as my best 9-hole score, a 2-under-par 34.

Although I was very happy with my improved scoring, I had major concerns about my swing, and decided, for the first time in my life, to seek help and take lessons. Now, if I could go back in time to the beginning after I moved back to the U.S., given how much time, energy and money I spent in my effort to improve my golf game, I probably would have invested money upfront working with a great instructor and built my swing properly from the beginning. I honestly believe that if I had done this, although I might not have become a tour pro, I at least could have become a solid scratch or near scratch golfer, because I would have avoided forming many bad swing habits and learned to execute a fundamentally sound swing with proper guidance and instruction.

Alas, that was not the course of action I chose, and so by the time I visited a well-regarded local teaching pro for help, there was already a ton of swing damage to undo. I attempted to faithfully follow the pro's instruction and do what he was trying to get me to do. However, so deeply ingrained were my bad swing habits that even though I hit as many as 500 balls per day working on the drills assigned by my instructor, I went from bad to worse once more, and was once again barely able to break 90 while attempting to swing like the pro wanted me to swing.

After a few lessons, I realized that I simply wasn't going to be able to change my swing like the instructor wanted me to no matter how many balls I hit, and so I abandoned my lessons. It wasn't necessarily that my teacher's instruction was faulty, but rather, my poor swing habits were so deeply ingrained that I simply wasn't physically able to alter my swing regardless of how much effort I put into trying.

Moreover, perhaps due to having intensified my swing practice during this period, I once again injured myself. This time I found myself with not only a newly developed lower back pain, but a nagging left shoulder injury as well. Once more, I found myself unable to hit a golf shot without significant pain.

It was too much for me. I had invested thousands of dollars and thousands of hours of time and energy into improving my golf game, and all I had to show for it was a broken body and a broken swing. I decided that the pursuit of golf just simply couldn't be worth all of this, and finally threw in the towel. For the second time in my life, I walked away from the game, this time, I told myself, forever!

Or so I thought. Once I decided to stop playing, I didn't play another round of golf or hit a single ball on the range or stroke a single putt on the practice green for well over two years. In place of golf, I took up martial arts as well as surfing. Over time, my body not only healed, but became much stronger.

Though I was no longer playing, I remained a fan of the game. I watched the major tournaments on TV. I also had a wedge lying around the living room, and occasionally I would chip on the carpet or take slow motion full swings with it in front of a full-length mirror.

This mirror practice soon became something of a routine, and I got into the habit of spending perhaps 10 minutes a day working on my grip, my set up, my alignment, and taking swings, initially in slow motion, as I monitored my form with the mirror. I noticed that the swing I was making in the mirror looked a lot better than the faulty swing I last played golf with. I didn't have that horrible over-the-top move or the extreme collapsed wrist that I previously was unable to fix no matter how hard

I tried. They say time heals all wounds, and it seemed as though my extended time away from the game had healed my swing flaws along with my physical pains, and I now had a clean slate to work with.

As I continued this daily ritual over the course of about two years, I began to wonder if this new swing I was making might not yield better results than before. I still didn't really want to get back into golf, but curiosity eventually overcame me, to the point where one day I decided to head over to the driving range and test it out.

At first I just took a pitching wedge and limited myself to a small bucket of balls. It took a few swings to get my timing down, but once I did, I was pleased to discover that my newly built swing was actually producing some very nice shots. I was now able to hit the ball with a nice controlled draw, and I even seemed to have more effortless power than before.

However, based on my previous failures I was hesitant to get back into a routine of beating balls and possibly developing poor swing habits or worse, injuring myself again. Therefore, I initially limited myself to one small bucket of balls every couple of weeks. The rest of the time, I continued to work on my swing at home in front of the mirror as I had been doing.

Of course, as all avid golfers know, golf is an incurable disease, and eventually I couldn't resist hitting more balls. I soon got into a routine of going to the driving range three times or more per week. However, I was careful to limit myself to no more than a small bucket, and to make sure that the core of my swing practice was my mirror work. My ball striking continued to improve, and I reached the point where I couldn't resist going back out on the course to see if I could produce the same quality of shots while actually playing a round.

I was pleased to discover that I could. Golf was suddenly fun again because now I was hitting the ball better than ever before. Instead of my former massive banana slice, I now was able to hit a gentle, controlled fade off the tee that more often than not found the fairway. My iron shots were now solid through the bag, even with my longer clubs. I was now hitting more greens than ever before. From tee to green, it was as if I had been reborn as a golfer.

I resumed playing golf in this way, although not nearly as frequently as before. I limited my golf to about once per month and no more than two or three trips to the driving range per week. However, even though I was enjoying golf more than ever before thanks to my newfound ball striking ability, I noticed something interesting: despite the fact that I was striking the ball far better than ever before, I wasn't scoring nearly as well as I had a few years earlier when my ball striking was terrible but my short game was sharply honed.

Despite my vastly improved ball striking, most of my scores were right around the mid to low 80s, and only rarely did I break 80. I figured that part of the reason for this was that I wasn't playing enough actual golf rounds. But I also knew that the true difference lay in my short game. While my ball striking had improved remarkably, my putting and short game had deteriorated significantly. I simply wasn't practicing these areas of my game, and it showed.

I couldn't help feeling dumbfounded by the mysteries and ironies of this game. Here I was, striking the ball round after round at a very high level yet barely able to break 80, while a few years ago, when my ball striking was barely above the level of a complete hacker, I was shooting in the 70s quite consistently.

As I pondered this mystery, at some point a light went on and suddenly I knew that I had discovered the True Keys to Breaking 80. Instead of the haphazard efforts with no real direction or understanding that had characterized my first three decades in golf, I finally felt that I had, for the first time since I began playing golf some 30 years ago, a true, fundamental and principle understanding of what was required to play good golf and break 80 consistently. I began to organize these principles, which I will teach you in this book, and put them into practice, and I have happily discovered that provided they are followed faithfully, these principles should enable any able-bodied golfer of even modest talent to improve in a linear, predictable manner and eventually gain the ability to break 80 consistently.

This book represents the culmination of my lifetime of trials and tribulations and triumphs and failures and ups and downs and hard knocks after more than 30 years of playing golf. My sincere hope is that in reading this book, you too will discover and embrace the true principles of breaking 80, so that you may avoid the arduous, frustrating and roundabout journey I took and instead enjoy the straight and (relatively) short path to maximizing your playing potential and enjoyment of the game, to the point where you too can experience and enjoy the pleasure of breaking 80, not just as a one-time fluke, but time and time again!

Part 1

Golf Myths and Conventions – Why You Can't Break 80

The Problem with How We Approach the Game of Golf

"Houston, we have a problem"

There is something wrong with the way we approach the game of golf. There has to be. How else can you explain how little the average golfer has improved, despite the incredible advances in equipment technology, despite the availability of high-speed video and swing analysis software, despite the availability of every conceivable piece of golf-related info on the Internet, including super-slow-motion swings of nearly every tour pro, and even despite the best efforts of the many good teaching pros who are sincerely dedicated to helping golfers improve? How can so much advancement in technology and availability of information result in so little progress in terms of improvement by the average golfer?

Let's begin by taking a look at some of the conventional ways golf is learned, taught and practiced, and why these conventions actually make it all but impossible for most golfers to break 80 consistently.

The Problem with Golf Instruction

Go to any driving range or practice tee in the world, and you'll likely encounter a scene similar to this one: a lesson pro set up at the corner of the range, giving a half-hour or full-hour lesson to a struggling golfer. Invariably, the scene unfolds as follows:

The lesson pro will ask the student to describe the state of his or her game, and then watch the student hit a few shots. The pro will proceed to point out flaws in the golfer's swing, often with the aid of a video camera and swing analysis software, and then attempt to fix the student golfer's swing flaws.

This teaching process tends to be similar for all golfers, including complete novices. The novice golfer will typically be asked to take a 7-iron, a 5-iron, or even a driver in some cases and the teaching pro will begin the process of "fixing" the invariably flawed swing.

The style of teaching and method of "fixing" the golfer will differ from teacher to teacher. In the most extreme example I have ever witnessed, I once watched a seasoned teaching pro with several decades of experience, who even claimed to have been a tour pro way back in the day, assault a brand new golfer with such a barrage of instructions that within the space of 15 minutes, the golfer was already hopelessly confused and barely able to take the club back for all the thoughts swimming around her head.

The lesson went something like this, all while the golfer was attempting to hit a shot:

"OK, now on the backswing, swing back low and slow, now cock your wrists as you rotate your shoulders, don't swing too far inside!, that a girl, keep your knees relaxed and bent, but don't bend your left arm!, keep the club on plane, now lead with your lower body, slide, don't spin your hips, shift your weight, don't release the club too early, now hit!, finish on your left side, that a girl....."

How much do you think the golfer improved under the guidance of this instructor? A mere 15 minutes into her golf career and she was already hopelessly confused and possibly scarred for life.

Some teachers employ a one-swing-fits-all approach. These instructors have a very rigid idea of what a proper swing looks like, and they attempt to get all of their students to swing in this way, whether or not the golfer is physically capable of doing so, or whether or not the swing method is appropriate for that particular golfer.

Better teaching pros are more selective in terms of the amount of information they impart at any one time and more flexible and adaptive to the needs and capabilities of each student and these teachers predictably achieve much better results.

Yet in all of these cases, the end result tends to be more or less the same. The golfer pays anywhere from $50 to $300 or even more for a half hour or full hour of instruction. He receives his lesson, and then he is basically left on his own to assimilate what he has learned, at least until the next lesson.

Do some golfers benefit from swing-tee lessons and become better golfers? Absolutely. Those golfers with the time and money and long-term commitment to take ongoing lessons with a capable instructor and assimilate those lessons with practice often show significant improvement both in terms of ball striking and scoring. And certainly, complete beginners at the game will almost always benefit from having a qualified instructor show them the basics of the swing and the game.

Before I go on, let me state up front that it is not my intention to bash the many capable teaching pros worldwide who are sincerely dedicated to helping golfers improve their games. Like any industry, some teaching pros are better and more dedicated to their craft than others, but in my observation, the cause of the ineffectiveness of golf instruction to improve the average golfer's handicap lies not with the intention or even the knowledge of the individuals who teach the game, but rather, the conventional, industry-standard approach to teaching. With that in mind, let's take a look at the way we learn how to play and how we approach improving at the game of golf.

Why Traditional Golf Lessons Usually Do Not Work

It would not be difficult to do a statistical survey of golfers who have taken lessons and get a precise picture of the effectiveness of those lessons. I'm sure you would find a large number of golfers that improved their ball striking and scoring as a result of taking lessons. However, I am equally certain that you would find at least as many golfers that reported that the lessons did not significantly improve their game, and I'd be willing to bet that you would find plenty more who responded that not only did they not improve as a result of their lessons, but that they actually got worse.

I believe that in most such cases, the poor results of golf lessons are attributable not to the teaching pro, but rather the teaching process itself. Some golfers only take a single lesson, when a series of lessons may be required to fully address their swing flaws and other weaknesses. Others take lessons but do not practice what they have been taught. Others want to take more lessons, but cannot afford to do so. Still others take lessons and do practice what they have been taught, but without the feedback of the instructor while practicing, the golfer ends up practicing the wrong things (the feel versus real syndrome), and in turn, ends up developing bad swing habits that lead to poor results.

The Problem with Swing-focused Instruction

There is still another even more important reason why I believe lessons tend to be ineffective in terms of improving golfers' overall performance: they are nearly all entirely swing-focused. We can all agree that the golf swing is an essential aspect of the game of golf. In order to hit full shots, we have to take a full swing at the ball, and our ball striking ability is ultimately determined by our grasp of and ability to execute a fundamentally sound swing.

However, despite the fact that the game we are playing is the game of golf, not golf swing, or even "ball strike," the majority of teaching pros teach the game as if the sole task of golf was to hit full-swing shots from a perfect lie on a driving range. Some even teach the game as though the sole task of golf was not even to produce functional, effective golf shots, but rather, to simply execute their notion of what an ideal swing motion should be. In other words, the teaching approach of many instructors is to focus on the minute nuances of the swing, even to the exclusion of consideration of the actual shots produced by the swing.

The reality of golf is that there is much, much more to the game than just the golf swing, or even just striking full shots. Moreover, as improbable as it may sound to you right now, as you will discover later in this book, most of these aspects of golf that do not even involve the full swing have a much greater impact on your ability to shoot lower scores than anything that is specifically full-swing related. Allow this thought to incubate in your mind as you read on.

Once again, the point I want to make here is not that full-swing instruction is not important or unnecessary, but rather, that the almost exclusive focus on full-swing instruction on the part of instructors and golfers alike to the exclusion of all of the other vital aspects of the game of golf is at best misguided, and at worst severely detrimental to enabling golfers who receive such instruction from realizing their full scoring potential.

The bottom line is that the approach to modern golf instruction, as it is currently taught, is by and large ineffective at best, a total failure at worst, and one need look no further than the average struggling golfer as evidence of this failure.

Information Overload

Today we live in the information society, where more information than ever before is instantly accessible, simply by turning on our TVs, computers or smart phones and doing a quick Internet search. This is certainly true when it comes to golf.

Nowadays we have every conceivable type of golf-related information available to us at the click of a mouse button. Like all information, however, there is good information and bad information and useful information and non-useful information. There is information that may apply for some people, but not others. It is not that having access to information is a bad thing. But we are all familiar with the expression: "too much information". Equally as harmful as bad information and too much information, from which results information overload, is otherwise good information that is not applied appropriately.

With this in mind, let's examine various types of golf information available to us, and how even seemingly good information can actually be damaging to one's golf game if not filtered carefully and applied appropriately.

Why Golf Tips are Ineffective

Every issue of Golf Digest and Golf Magazine and all of the other golf periodicals is packed with numerous golf "tips" from the best teachers and touring pros in the game. In fact, so enamored with tips are golfers that there is even a magazine called "Golf Tips"! Most golfers love tips, and are forever in search of that elusive swing tip that will fix his slice or add 30 yards to her drives.

Golf magazines are only too happy to oblige the public's demand for tips. In any given issue you'll find articles with titles like "7 tips for curing your slice" or "My 5 magic swing moves." Often, within the same magazine issue, you'll even find conflicting tips by different instructors that address the same problem.

Not only do golfers love receiving tips, but most golfers also love to give tips to others. As golfers we can't resist sharing the little tip we heard that somehow fixed our game, at least during the last round we played, and we love observing our fellow golfers and offering little swing pointers along the way. Most of us have a little inner Butch Harmon or Hank Haney inside of us that can't resist offering help to our fellow golfers, whether or not they need or solicit our advice or whether or not our advice is truly sound.

However, even with the best of intentions, the reality is that in most cases such golf tips are ultimately more harmful than helpful.

There are a few major problems with "golf tips." The first is that most are just jumbled, random pieces of advice that may apply to some golfers, but not most. The second problem is that at best, a "tip" will usually address one small aspect of a golfer's swing or game, which may or may not solve that issue, but almost certainly will not address the major issues with the golfer's game as a whole.

Lastly, tips tend to function as band aids, short-term remedies that may "work" for a day, or a round, but are seldom fundamental cures for the golfer's real weaknesses that are preventing him or her from playing better golf and shooting better scores on an ongoing basis.

At best, a golf tip may offer a short-term cure that may serve the golfer over the course of a round or two. At worst, a tip that may even technically be "right" for some golfers' issues may be completely wrong for the individual for whom it sounds like a good idea, who may implement it and actually ruin their round or even throw their entire game off as a result.

The bottom line is that golf tips will not provide lasting improvement and may even hamper your game, so you're much better off in the long run skipping past the golf tips in the golf magazines and fast forwarding through the Golf Channel lesson segments in search of more entertaining and less potentially damaging content.

If you can't resist reading up on these tips, or if you can't avoid being barraged by golf tips from friends and fellow playing companions, it is important that you apply an information filter and carefully weed out those tips that are actually useful from the majority of those that are potentially damaging to your golf game.

The Trouble with Training Aids

It seems as though every month there is a new infomercial on the Golf Channel advertising the latest odd-looking swing gadget that promises to groove a pure swing, eliminate slicing, add 30 yards to tee shots, and even cook your breakfast in the morning, all within the next six weeks or your money back!

How many of these training aids have you purchased? Are you a better golfer as a result? How many of these training aids have truly improved your golf scores? How many of these are now collecting dust in your garage?

The truth is that training aids vary in their function and effectiveness. Some do what they advertise, and the golfer may certainly benefit by using one or more training aid. For instance, the Speed Stick may in fact help you achieve a few more MPH of swing speed. The Momentus may indeed help you groove a better swing rhythm. The Tour Striker may indeed help you "hit down on the ball." A review of each training aid is beyond the scope of this book, but before you purchase your next training aid, here are a few kernels of truth you should know:

1) Beyond whatever functionality they may actually contain, the effectiveness that training aids promote is mostly hype. Next time you see an infomercial promising to increase your driving distance by 30 yards or take 7 strokes off your score within the next month, buy if you will, but make sure that you look beyond the nonsense hype and simply purchase the training aid on its own merit: that is, whether or not it appears that it might help that aspect of the game it was designed to improve.

2) Also be aware that most (but certainly not all) training aids are swing-focused aids, so even if they help you improve your swing, they may not necessarily improve your ability to score (despite the outrageous infomercial claims). As I have already suggested and as you will learn as you read on, most of the problems that the majority of training aids address are not the areas of the game that will significantly impact your ability to actually shoot better scores.

The Problem with Instruction Books & Videos

There are instruction books on the game of golf by nearly every top instructor, including Butch Harmon, David Leadbetter, and Hank Haney, as well as by many of the game's top players, including Jack Nicklaus, Nick Faldo, Tom Watson, and Tiger Woods.

Despite the fact that there is a wealth of sound information contained in many of these books, the truth is that even golfers who purchase, read and sincerely attempt to apply the principles within them more often than not do not improve significantly as a result.

The problem with instruction books is not necessarily the content, which may be excellent and highly informative, but with the inherent difficulty of translating written instructions into practice.

Additionally, the swing prescription of a particular book may not be precisely what you need for your golf game, and attempting to simply follow a set of swing descriptions or even photo sequences may actually leave your game in worse shape than it was before you began reading.

Perhaps the most famous example of a well-intended swing instruction book producing less-than-ideal results is the classic instruction book Five Lessons: The Modern Fundamentals of Golf by none other than the great Ben Hogan.

There may be no instruction book that goes into greater detail on the very basic fundamentals of the golf swing: the grip, the stance, the backswing, the downswing, and even the waggle! Moreover, this book was authored by no less than Ben Hogan, the person considered to be one of the very best ball strikers that ever lived. There are doubtlessly many golfers that have benefited from the lessons gleaned from this classic work.

However, Five Lessons is also notorious for having turned a generation of golfers who faithfully attempted to follow this instruction into hopeless slicers of the ball. You see, this swing method developed by Ben Hogan, who was plagued by hooks early in his career, was the precise prescription for his golf swing, but not necessarily the prescription for average golfers, the majority of who tend to have the opposite problem and suffer from slicing too much.

In fact, many of the top instructors in golf today have reinterpreted this work by advising golfers to adopt a stronger grip than the one advocated by the great Ben Hogan.

The point to be taken away here is that while instruction books can potentially be informative and helpful, the reality is that even the best instruction books by the best teachers and players in the game have not significantly improved the average golfer.

What is true about instructions books is equally true about golf instruction DVDs. There are golf instruction DVDs by most of the top instructors in the game, including David Leadbetter, Butch Harmon, and Hank Haney. There are also many "swing method" DVDs, such as the One-Plane Swing and the Stack and Tilt Swing.

Just as with instruction books, the problem with swing instruction DVDs is not the content and quality of instruction, which may be perfectly sound, but the issue of 1) whether or not the instruction offered is right for the student and 2) whether the student is able to assimilate the lessons and transfer the information successfully into his or her own game.

The reality is that in more cases than not, regardless of the soundness of instruction contained within instruction books and DVDs, most golfers are unable to properly assimilate that instruction, and most simply move on to the next shiny object with the same struggles and frustrations they had before.

The Problem with Golf Info on the Internet

Today, there is a wealth of golf information available on the Internet. A simple Google search will quickly turn up endless golf-related articles, websites, and golf forums packed with golf-related information. Perhaps of greatest value are the many super-slow-motion swing videos of the PGA tour pros now readily viewable on YouTube, which, for the first time in history, enable us to clearly see what is really happening in the golf swings of the world's best golfers.

As a result of this super-slow-motion video, many assumptions about the golf swing that were considered truths until very recently have been shattered. The result is a much clearer and more precise picture of what is actually happening throughout the swing and at impact in the golf swings of the best players of the game.

However, even with this highly valuable resource, the ability to observe the moves made in the best swings in the game does not necessarily translate into the average golfer's ability to perform them.

Furthermore, the same issue inherent in swing instruction books is equally true of swing videos. That is, what works for, say, Ernie Els, may not work for you. Every pro golfer has a unique swing that matches his or her body type, individual rhythm, and ball striking approach. The same is true for amateur golfers. While we certainly can and should attempt to study, understand and implement the fundamental moves made by the best players in the game into our own games, without a true understanding of what we are doing often times we ultimately end up doing more harm than good in our attempt to copy the swings of the pros.

Internet Golf Forums

Internet golf forums can be a valuable resource for sharing info about courses and equipment and experiences and even views about the golf swing. However, Internet forums by their nature are a collection of conflicting and often not-well-informed opinions, which can lead even a well-intended reader down a rabbit-hole of mind-boggling theory and confusion.

Therefore, if you choose to participate in golf forums, it is wise that you do so with a set of blinders and filters, so that you do not let harmful information seep into your stream of consciousness. By harmful information, again I mean that even though a particular swing opinion may be theoretically correct, it may not be correct for you, and attempting to implement what you read on golf forums, no matter how good that information may sound, may send you further spiraling on the endless merry-go-round of golf struggle and confusion.

The Problem with the Golf Channel

With the Golf Channel, golf fans now literally have 24/7 access to everything golf related. In addition to broadcasting golf tournaments and golf news, the Golf Channel programming is packed with instructional segments as well as many golf infomercials.

Some of this content is quite excellent. In fact, I highly recommend that all golfers watch the Playing Lessons from the Pros segments. In almost all of these segments, you will find the instruction focused on the thought processes of the pros as they navigate their way around the course, and this is information that really can help your game without doing more damage to your swing.

However, as with other forms of golf information, the golfer needs to take care to filter the useful information from the harmful information.

The difficulty here is that most struggling golfers are unable to distinguish between the two, and when it comes to assimilating swing information, the Golf Channel is no better than any other source of golf instruction, and due to the sheer volume and variety of information it delivers, without the ability to sift through and filter, an avid Golf Channel viewer may end up more confused than ever.

The bottom line is that with so much swing information available on the Internet and the Golf Channel, it is tempting to try to implement every tip and piece of swing advice you come across, the results of which can more often than not be detrimental to your game, if not downright disastrous.

How Golf Info Overload Can Hurt Your Game

The truth is that when it comes to the golf swing, there are many fundamentally sound, viable approaches, but the problem occurs when the golfer either attempts to adopt an approach not suited for him or her, or even worse, when the golfer attempts to try and implement every tip he or she comes across. Yesterday it was the one-plane swing, today it is stack-and-tilt, last year it was Natural Golf...

There is a vast amount of information on golf in general and the golf swing in particular instantly available on the Internet. One may assume that the more information, the better, but when it comes to golf, this is not necessarily true. This is because not all golf-related information is "good" information, and even if the information you are receiving is good information, it may not be compatible with other information you have likewise received.

For example, you struggle with slicing the ball and so you do a Google search that serves up hundreds of results related to fixing your slice. So now you click on a few of the results and begin trying out some of the ideas presented.

One site tells you that the problem is your swing plane. Another insists the problem is with your swing path. Yet another tells you that your grip is too weak. Still another site asserts that the problem is with your ball position. Yet one more site tells you that the problem with your slice is all between your ears. Then you visit a golf forum topic on slicing in which all of these opinions are clashing against each other within a single thread.

As you can see, even with just a single (albeit common) swing issue, there is an avalanche of advice. Each piece of advice may be fundamentally sound, but it may not be the prescription that you need. Furthermore, when you experience golf information overload, without a proper information filter in place every little tip and piece of advice you hear will seep into your stream of consciousness. You may unconsciously find yourself attempting to implement each tip you hear, often all at the same time, and the results can often be disastrous.

The bottom line is that whenever you access and process golf-related information, particularly as it relates to your swing, you must be very prudent in filtering out information that appears useful on the surface but which will not actually facilitate true improvement in your own game and which may ultimately do more harm than good.

Why Equipment & Technology Are Not the Answer

There is no question that today's equipment is highly advanced compared to that of yesteryear. Balls fly farther and straighter than ever before, and there is every conceivable game-improvement club on the market to assist golfers of all levels in maximizing their performance. Today's drivers and irons are much more forgiving than in the past. We now have forgiving game-improvement irons that produce acceptable shots from anywhere on the clubface, hybrid clubs that replace difficult-to-hit long irons, drivers with enormous faces and sweet spots, and even long putters to help us roll the rock better.

Yet even with these amazing advances in equipment technology, today's golfers still by and large continue to struggle to improve their games and shoot lower scores. While you can and certainly should take advantage of all of the help today's advanced equipment offers in order to get the most out of your game, it is clear that advances in equipment alone, impressive as they are, have not led to significant improvement to the tune of lower golf scores on the part of golfers overall.

Many struggling golfers make the mistake of believing that equipment alone is the solution to their golf problems. Many players are unable to stop themselves from buying every new driver and trying out every new iron set, constantly changing up what's in the bag in search of that one magical club that will transform their games.

There is no doubt that the right composition of properly fitting clubs can help most golfers play the game better, and to that end, I highly recommend that as part of your investment in this game, you spend the money to get a properly fitted set of clubs ideally tailored to your specific needs. However, once you have a set of clubs fitted to your unique specifications, please do not allow yourself to be distracted by the allure of promises by club makers that the latest club will transform your game. In the vast majority of cases, it won't.

The Problem with How We Approach Golf

As we have seen so far, the truth is that we simply do not approach golf in an optimal way. That is, we approach the game of golf in such a way that does not prioritize, and in some cases, does not even address our capacity to shoot lower scores. The conventional approach to improving at the game of golf is almost entirely focused on the nuances of the full swing, to the exclusion of every other aspect of the game.

The Two Games That Golfers Play

Although we think of golf as a single game, and in reality it is, within the single game of golf, there are at least two different games within the game that nearly all golfers play to some extent.

The Game of Golf Swing

The majority of today's golf instruction is swing-focused, if not downright swing-obsessed. It is therefore no surprise that golfers also tend to be swing-obsessed, at the expense of being target-focused and scoring-focused. Although on the surface such golfers are playing the game of golf, that is, even while they may tee up their ball and play holes and keep score, the game they are primarily focused on is the game of golf swing.

The game of "golf swing" involves the focus on and pursuit of a technically sound swing. On the practice tee, golfers playing this game are obsessed with hitting "positions" in the swing and concerned with how their swings look. Even while they are in the middle of a round of golf on the course, instead of being shot focused and target focused and strategy focused they are thinking about the position of their right elbow, their swing plane, their head movement, their weight shift, etc.

Theory versus Practice

Many golfers who play the game of "golf swing" are obsessed with the study of swing theory, and many of these golfers actually may have a very good theoretical "knowledge" of the swing. In fact, there are surely plenty of golfers well versed in swing theory who could probably deliver a college lecture on the golf swing, and not be terribly wrong about their theoretical knowledge. However, for just as many, when it comes to actually performing the golf swing and producing golf shots, many of these same golfers are simply unable to perform with their bodies what they know in their heads.

In contrast, there are PGA tour players and accomplished low-handicap golfers who routinely hit spectacular shots without really being able to tell you how they do so, any more than I can tell you how I am able to walk or ride a bike. For these players, in the course of their golf development, either through natural talent or effective guided instruction early on, they developed the ability to strike the ball purely, and simply do so without knowing or concerning themselves with the theory behind their ability, much as we can walk, run, toss a ball, and hit a tennis forehand accurately without really knowing the movement theory behind how we do these things.

This game of golf swing is the game played by most golfers who struggle continuously with the game, particularly ball striking. These golfers never get beyond the stage of golf development of thinking about and tinkering constantly with their swing, and never reach the point where they can forget about their swings and shift their focus to playing the game of golf as it was meant to be played.

Most high and medium handicap golfers fall into this category of players of the game of golf swing, but the reality is that all golfers play this game to some extent. How often have you heard even a PGA tour pro say something like: "I struck the ball fantastically but I didn't score worth a darn." When a golfer makes a statement like this, it reflects that golfer's tendency to view golf as two different games—one in which the object is to hit crisp, pure shots with picture-perfect swing motions, and the other in which the object is to shoot low scores by any means necessary.

The result of playing the game of golf swing will always be a sub-optimal scoring performance, simply because the golfer is focusing his or her attention on the wrong aspects of the game, which do not lead to the ability to produce his or her best possible scores.

The True Game of Golf

In contrast to the game of golf swing, the game that pros and successful low handicap golfers play is the true game of golf. Golfers who play the true game of golf leave behind whatever swing concerns they may have once they arrive on the first tee. From then on, they are focused on developing a strategy for the shot at hand, the hole at hand and even the overall round at hand, and executing that strategy.

Golfers playing the game of golf are focused on shot making. They are seeing the type of shot they want to play in the context of the challenge at hand presented by the course, and they focus on executing that shot.

Such golfers are likewise target focused. They are focused on a well-defined target that takes into account the obstacles presented by the given shot, and, mindful of the hazards that lurk, they pick out a precise target, devise a shot in their minds that will get them to that target, and then simply focus on executing the shot.

Such golfers are target focused and scoring focused. Golfers playing the game of golf have one objective in mind: shooting as low a score as possible. Therefore, these golfers navigate tactically around the course, and because they are scoring focused, the majority of their practice time is concentrated on where the scoring action is: the short game.

Such golfers know and adhere to the saying "drive for show and putt for dough." While they understand the importance of developing a complete game, they spend the bulk of their practice time improving their ability to sink putts from close range and lag long putts right up near the hole, and they hone their short games as well, knowing that even the best golfers in the game miss many greens and need to have the ability to scramble. They develop their wedge games too, knowing that a great wedge game can overcome many other shortcomings.

In short, golfers who play the game of golf are too busy playing the game to be overly concerned about the nuances of what's going on in their swings. If their ball flight is "off," they simply adapt during the round to their ball flight of the day, and put any fixes on the shelf until after the round.

Even on the practice tee, golfers who play the game of golf tend to be more target focused than swing focused. That is, even while practicing, they will likely have a precise target picked out, and will be focused on hitting shots at their target, rather than focused on some minor detail in their swing.

Contrast this approach to the golfer who plays golf swing, whose only target is the ball itself, and who has no concept of precisely where he is attempting to hit the ball and why, so concerned is he with the position of the head, the elbow, the right knee, and so forth.

Can you see how a simple shift in focus might lead to improved performance in terms of shooting lower scores? Which game of golf do you usually play?

Why Most Golfers Don't Improve through Practice

Most golfers realize that in order to improve their ability to play better golf and shoot lower scores, they need to work on their golf games and put in time practicing. There is no getting around it. Golf is a high-maintenance game, requiring the development of many different skills and many different types of shots in order to become a well-rounded golfer capable of consistently shooting low scores. Even the best golfers in the world spend hours each day on the practice tee and putting green honing their craft.

In order to become a well-rounded golfer, a player needs to become competent at all aspects of the game. Obviously the golfer needs to develop a swing that will produce consistent quality shots, but in addition, accomplished golfers must also be good putters, have decent short games, have the ability to get out of bunkers and other trouble, have the ability to navigate smartly around the course (sound course management), and also be able to manage their mind and emotions.

Given how demanding the game of golf is in terms of the broad skill set needed to shoot low scores, perhaps it is little wonder that the average golfer struggles to master this game. Most golfers have limited time to practice, and many golfers have no inclination to practice at all. Such golfers are recreational golfers, who are more or less content to go out and enjoy their afternoon on the course and hack it around as they enjoy a few beers and quality time with their buddies.

There is nothing wrong with being a recreational golfer and playing simply to get outdoors and enjoy time on the course with friends. However, this book is intended for those who want to be more than recreational golfers. It is intended for golfers who have a true desire to improve, and who are willing, committed and able to put in a reasonable amount of work on their golf games in order to improve.

Therefore, the rest of this book is written with the assumption that the reader wants to improve his or her golf game and is willing and able to commit a reasonable amount of well-directed time and effort toward that purpose.

The Problem with Swing-centered Practice

Just as we have already seen that most golf instruction is almost entirely swing-focused, the approach to practice of most golfers who actually work on their games is likewise almost exclusively swing-centered.

Go to any driving range in the world, and you will almost certainly see the same scene—lines of golfers pounding robotically away at buckets of balls. Most golfers, particularly higher handicap golfers, employ the "hit and rake" method, in which they hit their shot, and, barely looking up to see where it goes, quickly rake the next ball into position and repeat.

Likewise, by far the club that you will see being most used on the driving range is the driver. Most golfers simply can't resist pulling out their driver and seeing how far they can hit the big stick.

Most golfers hitting balls on the driving range have no real target. They simply line up in the same direction their mat or markers are pointing, and swing away.

If the practice tee has a putting green, most golfers at best spend only a token amount of time on it. Their putting practice will usually consist of dropping two or three balls down, slapping a few putts casually from hole to hole and hardly caring if the putts actually fall in or not. Invariably, after 5 or 10 minutes, most golfers get bored with putting and pack it up and go home.

Most golfers are even less likely to work on their short games. Short game practice for most high and mid handicap golfers is dull compared to hitting full shots, and most less-accomplished golfers, if asked, would probably tell you that it is more important that they work on their full swings than their short games.

The Practice Makes Perfect Myth

Range rats who routinely hit mountains of balls on the range tend to be adherents to the "practice makes perfect" ethos. Indeed, in most areas of life, the willingness to practice is reflective of a willingness to work hard to improve, and there is a direct correlation between the amount of sheer effort one puts forth and the positive results one achieves.

However, and this is an extremely important point for the golfer to grasp, in golf, the "practice makes perfect" ethos not only does not apply, but adhering to this mantra can actually have a reverse, highly detrimental result on the golfer's ability to ultimately improve.

As a golfer desiring to improve your game, it is imperative that you strike the words "practice makes perfect" from your vocabulary and rid yourself of this mentality as soon as possible.

Instead, you must replace "practice makes perfect" with a new mantra:

Practice Makes Permanent

Etch this statement into your memory and make it the High Truth around which you approach your work on improving your golf game. In golf, practice does not make perfect; practice makes permanent! This is particularly true when it comes to hitting balls on the driving range.

Why Hitting Balls Doesn't Lead to
Lower Scores

The truth about hitting balls on the driving range is that for most golfers, beyond a certain point, hitting balls is at best a waste of time with little impact on improving their games, and at worst, an exercise in futility that actually makes more golfers than not worse than they would be if they did not hit balls, not to mention an activity that leaves many ball beaters with aches and pains and even serious injuries.

I realize that this is a pretty radical statement, but allow me to clarify. It isn't that hitting golf balls is inherently bad, but rather, the manner in which most golfers approach hitting balls on the driving range is inherently ineffective, and in many cases, downright detrimental to their games.

How Your Golf Habits Determine Your Golf Destiny

You see, you may be surprised to learn that the thing that most separates low handicap golfers from high and mid handicap golfers is not talent, but rather, habits. In fact, allowing for the fact that the very best players in the game are blessed with enormous talent even beyond their fundamentally sound technique, what most separates the accomplished low handicap and scratch golfers from the rest of the golfing masses is simply this:

> *Accomplished golfers learn and ingrain fundamentally sound golf habits,*
> *while struggling golfers learn and ingrain fundamentally flawed golf habits*

The Swing Habit

As a brand new golfer, you likely had no idea how to swing in order to hit a golf ball when you first took up the game. You may have seen the pros on TV, or watched others around you and attempted to copy them. In fact, if you began learning golf with no guidance, you likely began hitting golf balls and then developed your swing through trial and error.

That's what most golfers do. They may take an introductory lesson or series of lessons to learn the bare basics, such as grip, stance, and swing, and maybe even some putting and short game instruction. However, for the vast majority of players, from that point forward the golfer forges ahead largely on his own, learning the game mainly through trial and error.

Many golfers who are highly motivated to play better golf commit to the ethos of practice makes perfect, and then commit to hitting bucket after bucket of balls on the range in search of swing perfection. For many such golfers, hitting balls becomes something of an obsession, and this breed of golfer mutates into a sort of hybrid golfer: a range rat.

What most of these golfers do not realize is that despite their positive intentions, in becoming range rats they are committing to a course of action that will more often than not ultimately have a detrimental effect on their game.

You see, when it comes to golf in general and hitting balls on the driving range in particular, practice makes permanent, not perfect. Therefore, imperfect practice results in permanent imperfection. Or to put it less politely, as you hit ball after ball, day after day, week after week, year after year on the driving range, you are not improving. Rather, you are simply ingraining your existing motion and making it your deeply ingrained swing habit.

If you are doing this with a fundamentally flawed swing, those flaws not only will not go away as a result of hitting more and more balls, but the exact opposite will occur. The more you practice with a fundamentally flawed motion, the more those flaws become deeply ingrained, to the point where fixing a fundamentally flawed swing that has been deeply ingrained as a result of hitting many thousands of balls becomes a most difficult task to accomplish.

Little Pros

The World Junior Golf Championship is held every year in San Diego, where I live, and every year the world's best junior golfers gather to compete. One of the age-group events is held at a course I sometimes practice at, so every year I have the opportunity to watch the best junior golfers in the world practice in preparation for the tournament.

These kids are amazing golfers. The winning score on some pretty tough courses is usually under par for most of the age groups, and every year I see many scrawny young kids who are not yet even close to full grown smashing 280 yard drives and hitting the ball like little pros. Even their mannerisms are eerily similar to those of PGA touring pros.

In watching these amazing golfers year after year, I have come to realize something significant. Most of these young golfers are not necessarily superior athletes. That is, their high skill level is most definitely NOT due to being exceptionally athletic or coordinated. Rather, their high skill level is the result simply of having ingrained fundamentally sound golf habits from the very outset of their young golfing careers, usually under the watchful eye of a father or club pro who is highly vested in developing the young golfer's game.

Indeed, I am friends with the family of one such little pro, who at the ripe old age of 11, is already a near-scratch golfer who has won numerous junior tournaments. This young golfer has practiced under the guidance of a teaching pro since the age of 2, and each year the family invests no less than the equivalent of an average adult's annual salary in developing his talents.

This little pro and others like him are perfect positive embodiments of what I said earlier about practice making permanent. These golfers are the product of perfect, precise practice from the outset of their golfing lifetime, which results in fundamentally sound, permanent habits that will enable these fortunate few golfers the ability to play golf at the highest level throughout their golfing lives.

For the rest of the golfing population not so fortunate to have been born into a position to be developed as a little pro, however, the outlook is not so rosy, and as a result of imperfect, imprecise practice from the outset of their golfing lifetime, the inevitable outcome is fundamentally flawed and permanent habits that makes it all but impossible for the unfortunate masses to develop the ability to play golf at a high level throughout their golfing lives.

Why Most Golf Injuries Occur

Now, a bit more about beating balls on the range. Many avid golfers, including professional golfers, suffer from chronic back, neck and shoulder pains. Most of these injuries, however, do not occur as a result of playing rounds of golf. Rather, most golf-related injuries occur through the sheer repetition of pounding balls on the driving range. Avoidance of injuries is just one more reason to be prudent in your approach to practicing golf. When it comes to golf practice and improvement, despite conventional wisdom which says in order to become good at golf you need to hit thousands of balls on the range, quality of practice absolutely trumps quantity!

The True Keys to Scoring

If there are so many issues with traditional forms of instruction, sources of golf information, and even how golf is conventionally practiced, how does one actually go about improving his or her ability to score? Well, let's take a look.

Why Putting and Short Game are King

When it comes to the task of shooting low scores in golf, putting and the short game are what it is all about. By far the biggest difference between struggling high and mid-handicap golfers and low handicappers who have the ability to break 80 consistently is a difference in short game proficiency.

Simply put: if you do not have at least reasonable proficiency in the short game, you will forever struggle to maximize your ability to shoot low scores, regardless of your level of ball-striking ability. The reasons for this are actually quite straight forward and logical.

Despite most golfers' almost exclusive dedication to the swing and ball striking, the fact is that as many as two-thirds of all shots played in a round of golf are played from 100 yards and in. Over one-third of all shots in any given round are putts, and over half of all shots played in most rounds of golf are played from 20 yards from the hole and closer.

So despite the fact that almost all instruction on the part of teachers and almost all practice effort on the part of golfers is focused on the full swing, the reality of golf is that the majority of shots in golf do not even require a full swing! Is it any wonder then that the average golfer struggles mightily to break 80, when the pros that teach the game and the golfers that practice it all but ignore any effort to become proficient at the majority of the shots actually required to play the game?

I believe there are a number of reasons for the lack of due attention given to those aspects of the game of golf on the part of teachers and practitioners alike. Most golfers simply have more fun practicing full shots than they do short shots and putts. Many golfers consider putting practice to be tedious and boring. It can also be difficult to find access to a good short game practice area. However, the primary reason for negligence of short game practice may be one that most people do not consider.

Beyond all of the reasons I listed above, I believe that golf instruction and practice is almost exclusively full-swing centered simply because of the illusion that since shots played with the full swing cover about 90% of the distance of any given hole, these shots also must represent 90% of the importance of scoring. In other words, I believe that subconsciously, golfers have a tendency to equate the relative importance of a shot with the distance covered by that shot.

Golf is a Target Game

In fact, not only is the overwhelming majority of all shots played in a round of golf short game shots involving less than a full swing, the relative impact of these shots on your golf score is much higher than that of longer full shots. By some estimates, 80% of your handicap can be attributed to the various elements of the short game: pitching, chipping, greenside bunker play, and putting.

In his excellent Short Game Bible, short-game and scoring guru Dave Pelz even went so far as to assert that if the average 10- to 12-handicap golfer developed a "scratch" level short game, that player's overall handicap would drop to between 2 and 4!

In other words, as a general rule, the closer you are to the hole, the greater the impact that shot will have on your overall score. There are clear reasons for this, which I will discuss in much more detail later on.

For now, let me ask you a quick question:

If in fact it is true that as much as 80% of your handicap is attributable to the short game, are you currently spending 80% of your practice time working on these aspects of your game? Are you spending even 75% of your time, or even 50% of your time working on your short game? Are you even spending 10% of your time working on your short game???

Golf is inherently a target game. What most golfers fail to realize is that the actual target expands and contracts and changes with each shot, and that the level of precision required also varies depending upon the shot, and thus the target, at hand.

As an example, let us look at the two extremes of golf shots: the drive and the 3-foot putt. For most drives, perhaps excepting a few unique holes that are dauntingly narrow and surrounded with OB and water and only provide the tiniest of landing areas, there is normally considerable margin of error for a miss. Most often, even if the golfer does not hit his drive smack dead in the middle of the fairway, a less-than-perfect drive will still leave the golfer with a very good opportunity to make par on the hole. A drive can find the rough and still be well within play. A drive can be hit imperfectly and lack full distance, but the golfer still has a shot to the green. Even a completely miss-hit drive does not eliminate the possibility that the golfer can make par. For instance, if the golfer drives the ball into the trees, even if he doesn't have a direct shot to the green he can still pitch out into the fairway, hit his next shot on the green, and possibly hole his putt for par.

The point is that when it comes to driving, the actual target area that at least minimally fulfills the function of the shot is actually quite large. For most golfers playing a 400 yard hole, this may be a distance range of from 225~275, with an allowable directional miss of up to 40 yards or even more, depending on the hole. And because it is possible to recover from a poor drive, even drives that are not hit within the above parameters may function well enough to enable the golfer to still make par, or at least no worse than bogey. Only the worst complete miss-hits or drives that land in a hazard or OB may result in clear strokes added to one's score for the hole.

The 3-foot putt, in contrast, offers practically zero margin for error. There is only one goal of a 3-foot putt: to hole that putt. No other outcome is acceptable. Since the hole is slightly larger than the ball, the golfer may hit the ball a couple centimeters off line and still hole the putt. However, any offline hit greater than this will ensure a miss, and one additional stroke added to the scorecard with no possibility of recovery.

The point of this brief example is to demonstrate the fact that golf is a target game, and that the size of the target expands and contracts depending upon the shot to be played. For drives, the target may be a very wide circle encompassing the fairway and even the rough as wide as 50 yards in diameter. For an approach shot, the target may be the circumference of the green, or it may even include an area just off the green that offers a relatively easy chip to the hole. For a long chip shot or a short pitch shot, the target may be an 8-foot circle surrounding the hole. For a lag putt, the target may be a 3-foot circle surrounding the hole. And finally, for a short putt, the target will almost always be the hole itself.

As the golfer gets progressively closer to the hole, the target area becomes progressively smaller, but there is more to the story. Not only does the target area become progressively smaller, but the negative impact on the score of not successfully hitting the ball within that target area grows proportionally.

The Importance of Course Management/Strategy

After the short game, the next most important aspect of golf is undoubtedly course strategy (course management); that is, the conscious thought process the golfer employs to navigate intelligently around the course.

Indeed, for most high- to mid-handicap golfers, course management may be even more important than ball striking proficiency when it comes to shooting low scores.

Course management could be called the art of managing your misses. Even the great Ben Hogan, considered perhaps the greatest on-course strategist that ever played the game, stated that golf is a game of managing one's misses.

The reality is that even PGA Tour pros seldom hit perfect shots. For rank amateurs, hitting perfect shots is even less common. Therefore, in golf, every shot hit requires thought about where the ball might end up if the shot doesn't come off as planned.

This is not to suggest that the golfer should approach each shot with a negative attitude of defeatism. Rather, he or she simply needs to accept the reality that most shots, particularly full shots, are not going to land exactly where one plans them to land, and therefore plan for such contingencies.

Actually, provided the golfer grasps the concept of golf being a target game, in which the target expands and contracts in a manner roughly proportional to the distance and overall difficulty of the shot at hand, then course management becomes not so much about managing misses, but rather, managing targets.

As an example, imagine you are in the middle of the fairway facing a shot of 150 yards, with the pin tucked in the front left portion of the green and guarded on the front left side by a bunker. A small pond also lurks to the left of the green. What is your target?

All too often, a high-handicap golfer will zone in on the pin, take his 7-iron, and fire right at the flag. For such a golfer, whenever he faces an approach shot to the green, his default target is the pin, without giving even passing consideration to the dangers that lurk nearby.

Such a golfer is unaware of the concept of expanding and contracting targets, and is therefore unaware that automatically establishing "the pin" as the target for a 150-yard approach shot is simply unreasonable and is usually not prudent.

A quick glance at the Shotlink statistics on PGAtour.com will back up this assertion. Even for PGA Tour pros, the very best golfers in the game, the average distance for approach shots in the 125 – 150 range in 2011 was about 22 feet, or just over 7 yards. For amateurs, obviously this distance range will be considerably broader.

Therefore, the prudent golfer, armed with a realistic accuracy picture for any given shot he faces, will pick out a reasonable target range that takes into account the laws of probability.

In the case of our example above, you would be wise to forget about the pin and pick a much broader target. Taking into account the bunker left-front of the green that guards the pin and even more trouble in the form of a small pond to the left of the green, you might choose a target that covers about a 10-yard area from the middle of the green to the right side of the green. If you hit the ball as planned, you'll leave yourself with a medium-length putt. But even if you miss your center target, if you go right you'll leave yourself with plenty of green to work with, and even if you go left, you might find yourself (accidently) right near the hole. Only a complete yank or hook to the left will leave you in serious danger.

Contrast this approach with the golfer who takes dead aim at a well-guarded pin. Too often, for every shot that comes off as planned, that golfer will wind up short in the bunker, left in the pond or short sided at least as many times, and the result of those misses will invariably be Big Numbers that ruin otherwise good rounds far more often than pulling off the perfect shot will result in a birdie.

The lesson here is that there is a prudent strategy for every shot that is dictated by the size of the realistic target demanded by that shot, and by taking even just a moment to think and plan each shot based on the appropriately sized target, the average high and mid handicap golfer will be amazed at the number of strokes that can be saved by nothing more than better decision making.

There is actually considerable margin of error when it comes to most full-swing shots. As the golfer gets closer to the hole, however, the margin for error narrows, which is still another argument for investing more time in the short game rather than the full swing!

This concludes the first part of this book. In Part 1, we lifted the veil of many of the conventional myths and assumptions about the game of golf to reveal the real truths about the game and identify those conventions that inhibit golfers from realizing their true scoring potential and prevent you from being able to break 80. Hopefully you can now see how some of these factors may be inhibiting your own golf progress, particularly your ability to shoot lower scores. In Part 2, it is now time to get down to the business of examining the True Keys to Breaking 80, and learning exactly what we need to do to gain the ability to become consistent 70s shooters ourselves.

Part 2

The True Keys
to Breaking 80

You Can Break 80!

Despite all of the statistical data to the contrary, and even despite your own golfing experience to date, breaking 80 is in fact a goal that is attainable by any able-bodied golfer of even modest talent who is willing to put forth a reasonable amount of intelligently focused effort into one's game.

As you will soon discover, the difficulty of breaking 80 lies not so much within the task itself, but rather, the conventional approach espoused almost universally throughout the golf industry that makes the task of breaking 80 all but impossible for most golfers.

No less a genius than Albert Einstein once said:

"Insanity is doing the same thing over and over and expecting different results"

In Part 1 of this book we have already examined the ineffective things that most golfers do over and over again with the expectation of improvement, but with the inevitable result of frustration born of lack of progress. We already know that for most golfers, conventional golf instruction simply does not work. We know that the latest advances in equipment technology do not significantly improve scores. We know that endlessly beating golf balls on the driving range does not lead to tangible improvement. And we know that access to hordes of golf-related information does not necessarily result in better golf scores.

So if these things do not work in terms of improving our ability to shoot better scores and play better golf, what does? What does good golf truly entail, and how can we finally become a good golfer ourselves, one capable of consistently shooting low scores in the 70s?

Before we discuss precisely how to play good golf, we need a working definition of "good golf" that we can actively strive toward.

What is "Good Golf"?

What is "good golf" anyway? Surely to a golfer who has never broken 100, a round of 98 will certainly feel like he or she has played "good golf" or even "great golf." The same would be true for the golfer that cards an 89 but who had previously never broken 90.

Some golfers do not even equate good golf with their score. Even tour pros will often comment at the end of their round that they "played great but didn't score well." Indeed, it is certainly possible to hit the ball great and yet still come away with a relatively poor score. And conversely, we have probably all had those rounds where we hit the ball all over the place but still somehow managed to produce a respectable score, with the end result being that we felt like we "played poorly but scored well."

Even though from our examples above we can clearly see that "good golf" is most often in the eye of the beholder, for the purpose of our mission to gain the ability to break 80, I would like to propose a somewhat more objective working definition of "good golf" that we, as students of the game, can use to base our progress and performance on moving forward.

My new definition of good golf is what I believe to be the minimum level of scoring capability that any golfer of even modest natural talent who applies oneself should feel comfortable striving to achieve. So what exactly is my working definition of "good golf"?

Is Bogey Golf "Good" Golf?

Is bogey golf "good golf"? Bogey golf means that given a par 72 golf course, a golfer will play his round in roughly 18 strokes over par, or one stroke over par per hole, for a score of about 90.

Given that bogey golf is considerably better than the worldwide average golf score of 97, this doesn't sound too bad. However, it is still a full 10 strokes higher than our stated goal of breaking 80. In truth, bogey golf implies that the golfer, on average, makes one stroke-costing mistake on every hole he plays.

I believe that bogey golf should NOT be an ultimately satisfactory level of golf for any able-bodied golfer with a desire to improve and realize his or her potential. Surely we can do better than to average one significant mistake on each and every hole?

Obviously a golfer currently struggling to break 100 may want to set bogey golf as an intermediate progress point along the way to maximizing his or her potential. But I want you, the reader, to ultimately become much better than just a bogey golfer.

Is Par Golf a Realistic Goal?

What about par golf? If bogey golf is not particularly accomplished golf, should we not strive to play par, or scratch, golf? Par golf implies that for a par 72 golf course, the golfer, on average, shoots a round of 72.

On the surface, it makes sense that since golf courses were presumably designed with a particular par in mind, the expectation is that golfers should reasonably be able to play par golf.

Of course we all know that this is not the case. The truth is that of all golfers who carry an official handicap, less than half one percent are scratch golfers or better (source USGA).

What this suggests is that par, or scratch golf, is certainly not at all close to "average" golf, and it further suggests a very elite level of play. In fact, par golf, by definition, is "flawless golf." Now, this does not imply that a golfer who shoots a round of even par played every shot perfectly, hitting every fairway and every green and two-putting each green. Rather, it does imply that, over the course of the round, the golfer countered each mistake (a bogey or worse) with a remedy (birdie or better), and otherwise navigated each hole and the course overall in such a way as to match the standard of par.

The ability to play par golf implies a complete golf skill set: the ability to hit solid, controlled drives a reasonable distance and keep the ball in play off the tee, the ability to hit solid iron shots that consistently land on or very near the green, the ability to putt, chip and pitch the ball, as well as the ability to strategize intelligently, keep one's emotions in check, and most of all, to do all of these things with enough consistency while avoiding any serious round-killing misses along the way so as to enable such a golfer to regularly shoot a score of right around even par.

When it comes to PGA tour pros, these elite players are not merely scratch golfers: they are plus-handicap golfers. That means that they play a level of golf that is beyond flawless. So refined are their talents and skills that they are routinely able to perform even better, on average, than the par of a course.

If you have ever seen a tour pro play golf in person at a PGA Tour event, you will know instantly that these golfers are on a completely different level than even solid low handicap or scratch golfers. If you watch them warming up on the practice tee, you'll see that their swings are all perfectly rhythmic and that they rarely ever hit a shot off line. Their swings produce a different level of swing speed and their level of precision with all shots in their bag is beyond even the comprehension of most amateurs.

Few golfers are able to attain such a level without a combination of serious natural talent and time and commitment to the game, not to mention financial investment and guidance in the form of coaching and instruction from the outset of their golfing careers at a very early age.

Clearly par golf or better implies not only a highly accomplished level of golf, but an extraordinary dedication to working to achieve this level as well. Given the extremely small number of golfers capable of reaching this level, for most high and mid handicap golfers with limited talent, time and resources, the goal of playing par golf is clearly not a reasonable goal.

New Definition of Good Golf

I believe that a round of golf of 80 or better is a level of "good golf" that most serious golfers should reasonably strive for and can definitely achieve provided they have a reasonable willingness to practice along with a sensible game plan for improving.

Why do I say that shooting 80 or better specifically implies good golf?

Well, we have already seen that bogey golf is indicative of one mistake per hole on average. Likewise, we have seen that par golf implies essentially mistake-free golf. Given a par 72 golf course, a round of golf that is midway between bogey golf (18 over par) and par golf (zero over par) would be a round of nine over par, or 81.

A round of 81 on a par 72 golf course means that, on average, we make 9 pars and 9 bogeys. In other words, in order to shoot an 81, on average, we play 9 holes flawlessly, and make a single stroke-costing mistake on the other 9 holes.

Of course not every round of 81 unfolds so precisely. A double bogey may be offset by a birdie, or a couple extra pars. Even holes on which we make a par, perhaps we hit a wayward drive or miss a green but recover with a nice chip shot or a score-saving short putt. But as a simple measure, we can say that a round of 81 is exactly halfway between flawless par golf and mediocre bogey golf.

If we can simply manage a round that works out to one more par than bogey, this brings our score down to 80. This means playing a round that works out to making 10 pars and 8 bogeys. And if we can somehow manage to do just one better than that, this will bring us to our goal of breaking 80, with a score of 79.

Therefore, given that shooting a round of 80 means that we were able to play more good holes than bad holes and make more pars than we did bogeys, I believe that implies that we have played a respectable round of "good golf."

Moreover, I believe that this level of golf is highly attainable for the average golfer. If we break down what it means to shoot a round of 80, we can see that we can still make a stroke-costing mistake on almost half of all 18 holes and still manage to shoot 80. If we can somehow manage to squeeze one birdie or just one extra par into the mix, that will give us our magical round of 79, and thus, the accomplishment of breaking 80.

As we can see, shooting 80 or even 79 does not require that we play perfect golf. There is still plenty of room for error in producing such a score. Furthermore, you will soon discover that the skill set for producing such scores does not even require a perfect or necessarily even highly accomplished level of ball striking. What breaking 80 does require, rather, is a focus on the principles of scoring, which we will soon discuss in much greater detail.

Having broken down and taken a close look at what shooting a round of 80 or 79 entails, can you now begin to picture this level of play as something that is within the realm of possibility for you as a golfer?

In fact, as you read on, you will soon see that with the proper approach, I will show you how the ability to shoot 80 or better and consistently play "good golf" is a level of play that is well within your reach!

How to Play "Good Golf" and Break 80

Now that we have a working definition of "good golf," we can turn our focus to the all-important question of precisely how we go about playing good golf and developing the ability to shoot 80 or better consistently.

Before we do so, I would like to introduce you to my new theorem of scoring in golf, which will become the basis of our approach to developing the ability to break 80 consistently.

New Theorem of Scoring in Golf

The closer the shot is to the hole, the greater the negative impact not fulfilling the function of that shot will have on the player's score

What does this mean in practical terms? It means that the farther one is from the hole, the greater the margin for error and greater the level of forgiveness for a miss and conversely, the closer one is to the hole, the smaller the margin of error and smaller the level of forgiveness in terms of impact on the score.

To put it even more simply, this theorem says that a missed 3-foot putt will impact your score more than a wayward drive will. A lag putt that finishes 8 feet from the hole instead of within 3 feet will impact your score more than a skulled fairway wood shot. A flubbed chip will impact your score more than missing the green with your iron approach shot will.

To spin this theorem around in positive terms, it can also be interpreted to say:

> *The closer the shot is to the hole, the greater the positive impact fulfilling the function of that shot will have on the player's score*

So from this viewpoint, the theorem also says that the better we can get at the shots in golf that are played from relatively close distances to the hole (putts, chips, pitches, greenside bunker shots), the more we will improve our score, whereas even as we improve at those shots played farther away from the hole (full-swing drives and irons), our improvement of these shots will have less impact on our ability to score than our improvement on shots played closer to the hole.

Take a moment to digest this concept, and consider how embracing it might change your approach to improving your own game.

What it comes down to is that for high and mid-handicap golfers, or in other words those golfers who are not yet breaking 80, intelligently focused short game practice produces a much greater return on investment (ROI) of time and effort and even money spent playing and practicing in terms of scoring improvement compared to beating balls on the range or focusing on improving the nuances of the golf swing.

Need more convincing? Consider that around 35~40% of all shots played in a round by most golfers are putts, and over 50% of all shots played over the course of a round of golf take place within about 20 yards of the green.

Beyond the sheer ratio of shots played on or near the green, there is another compelling reason why these shots are so much more important to be proficient at, which is right in line with our Theorem:

The short game is where scoring in golf occurs

What does this mean? Well, let me ask you a simple question:

From what distance do you normally actually hit the ball into the hole?

Obviously one almost never holes out a drive. How about your approach shot to the green? In my golfing lifetime I have had two hole-out eagles, as well as two hole-in-ones. That's more than a lot of people, but overall it is not a lot of hole-outs. What about wedge shots from, say, 50 to 75 yards from the green? I've holed out a few of these as well, but most of these shots also typically do not find the bottom of the cup. What about greenside pitches and chips? Most experienced golfers who have played long enough have holed out a handful of these, but it certainly isn't something that happens with any consistency, even among tour pros.

So that leaves us on the green. Clearly, it is from the green, putting, that we actually hit the ball into the hole. But that is not the end of the story. When it comes to actually holing out your shot, all putts are most definitely not created equally. There is a vast difference in the percentage of putts holed from close range verses those holed from longer distances.

Let's take a look at the putting performance of PGA Tour pros according to the Shotlink statistics from the pgatour.com website for the year 2011. From within 3 feet from the hole, tour pros make nearly every putt they attempt, at around 98%. From 4-8 feet, this figure drops to just below 70%. From 5-10 feet from the hole, the percentage goes down to about 50%, and even from as close as 10-15 feet from the hole, the percentage of makes drops even further, to only around 30% or so. From beyond 25 feet from the hole, even the very best players in the world barely make 5% of their putts.

What do these figures tell us? The message is clear: your best chance to reasonably hole out a putt, and therefore save a stroke, is from close range, or about 15 feet and in. The range from which the very best players in the game consistently hole out their shots is our best indicator of what is reasonably, and statistically, possible for us.

In other words, if the very best golfers who have ever played the game are unable to consistently hole out putts from beyond 15 feet from the hole, playing usually on the best green conditions, there is no expectation that we amateurs and less-talented golfers should do better.

Similarly, since we do statistically have a very good probability of making shots from within this range, the impact on your overall score of missing a shot from a distance where a make is statistically highly probable is significant.

It is important to recognize that these statistics represent the percentages of the best players in the world. The make percentages from the same distances for high and mid handicap golfers, and even many low handicap golfers, are considerably lower than these figures!

However, there is much more to the story. Above, I asked you from what distance you and most golfers consistently hit the ball into the hole, and we have seen that the clear answer to this question is from close-range putts.

Now here is another question:

From what distance do you normally hit your ball close to the hole?

Let's take a look at the distances from which PGA tour pros are able to consistently hit shots to within the range we established above from which it is statistically possible to hole a high percentage of putts.

When chipping from the fringe, pros are able to get the ball, on average, to within right around 3 feet of the hole. When playing a shot within 10 yards of the hole, they are consistently able to get the ball within 4 feet. From 10-20 yards, they are able to get the ball right around within 6 feet of the hole. From 20-30 yards as well as from greenside bunkers, pro shots on average land just within 10 feet. And from beyond 30 yards, even the very best golfers in the world begin to have trouble consistently landing the ball even to within 12 feet of the hole.

As we can see from these numbers, it is only from relatively short distances and with shots played with less than full swings that the best players in the world are able to consistently hit their shots to within the range from which it is statistically possible to then hole out a high percentage of putts.

We can now see from our analysis above that it is with longer putts, chips, and greenside pitches that we can consistently hit the ball to within a range that offers a high probability of holing out our next shot. And we also know that it is with short-range putts that we can consistently hit the ball into the hole with high proficiency.

Based on the above, it is clear that the true key to scoring in golf is twofold:

1) Hit the ball within the high-percentage hole-out range

2) Make putts from our high-percentage hole-out range

This combination of hitting an approach shot close to the hole and then hitting a putt from short range into the hole represents our one-two scoring punch that will most directly lead to true improvement to the tune of lower scores on your scorecard.

Our New Theorem of Scoring tells us that makes or misses (that is, fulfilling the function of the shot) within this range will have a higher impact on our score than shots beyond this range.

Indeed, while the function of shots within our True Scoring Range is scoring, the purpose of all shots beyond our True Scoring Range is simply positioning.

In reality, every type of shot in golf, from drives, to approach shots, to pitches, to chips and to putts, has its own specific function. Therefore, before we go further let us take a look at each basic shot type in golf along with its function and value in terms of its impact on scoring.

Analysis of Shot Values and Functions

Function of Drives

As we already determined earlier, the objective of hitting a drive off the tee is obviously not to hit the ball into the hole. It then stands to reason that our target for the drive is considerably larger than the size of the hole. In fact, on most tee shots we have considerable margin for error. We can often be far from perfect in our ball contact or direction, and still succeed in putting the ball in play.

Indeed, the true function of drives is simply positioning. All we are trying to do with our tee shots on par 4 and par 5 holes is to put the ball in play in a position that gives ourselves the easiest possible next shot.

We do not need to land the ball on a dime in the middle of the fairway. We don't even necessarily need to be in the middle of the fairway, or even the fairway at all. In fact, even PGA tour pros miss plenty of fairways. Joe Durant, the very best driver on tour in 2011 in terms of accuracy, still only hit about 3 out of 4 fairways. Middle of the pack drivers did considerably worse, at just over 60%, while a number of successful golfers, including Phil Mickelson, Jason Day, Ryan Palmer, and Aaron Baddeley, barely hit the ball in the fairway over 50% of the time!

Despite the fact that these golfers are far from perfect in terms of driving precision, they are still capable of shooting great scores and playing amazing golf. This clearly shows that when it comes to driving, there is considerable margin for error. If the golfers referenced above can consistently break par while only hitting half of all fairways, clearly we need not even do this well in order to achieve our stated goal of breaking 80.

What about driving distance? It is true that the very best players in the world hit the ball a long way. However, PGA winners including Jerry Kelly, Brian Gay, Chris DiMarco, Kevin Na and Zach Johnson barely average more than 270 yards on their drives. For amateurs who typically play much shorter courses, there is no need to hit the ball even that far.

Excellent driving certainly does not require that you hit the ball dead straight. In fact, most of the best golfers in the world have a preferred ball flight, and work the ball considerably either left or right.

Lee Trevino, one of the best drivers and ball strikers to ever play the game of golf, hit a big cut on virtually every shot. Rocco Mediate and Kenny Perry are examples of highly successful golfers who play a big draw on just about every shot they hit. I've played with golfers who aim their banana slice 50 yards left and consistently hit the ball in the fairway and still manage to break 80 consistently (in fact, I used to be one such golfer myself; I've since gained control over my slice and nowadays I still usually aim down the left side of the fairway and hit a nice, controlled cut shot on just about every drive I hit).

The point is that you do not need to be precisely accurate, prodigiously long, or even a perfectly straight ball striker in order to be a decent driver of the golf ball and produce drives that will still give you a great opportunity to break 80.

The true function of driving is simply to advance your ball down the fairway at a distance and from a position that enables you to hit your next shot on or near the green (in the case of par 4s) or further down the fairway in position to get the following shot on or closer to the green (in the case of par 5s).

As you will learn later on in this book, successful driving is as much about on-course strategy and how you think about and plan your tee shot as it is actually hitting it.

Function of Approach Shots

We have established above that the primary function of drives is positioning, and that the target range for most drives is relatively large, with considerable room for error.

What about the function of approach shots then? Here, we define an approach shot as any full-swing shot hit with the intent to hit the ball on the green. Therefore, approach shots normally consist of second shots into par 4 holes, third shots into par 5 holes (sometimes second shots when going for the green in two), and tee shots on par 3 holes.

What is your target once you are facing an approach shot where you have "enough club" to reach the green? Is your primary target the pin? Is it the green? Or is it simply somewhere in the vicinity of the green?

The actual answer is (or should be): it depends. Even for PGA tour pros, there is a considerable difference in their accuracy level from approaches from 100-125 yards (around 20 feet from the pin on average), approaches from 150-175 yards (around 26 feet) and approaches from 200-225 yards (around 40 feet).

There is also a significant difference between the percentage of greens that tour pros hit on average from the fairway (over 75%) and from rough and fairway bunkers (around 50%).

Of course we also know that the average golfer is not nearly as accurate as a PGA tour pro. Therefore, the lesson here for approach shots is twofold:

1) For most full-swing shots, given the expected margin of error (average distance from the pin), establishing the pin as your primary target is not reasonable

2) The farther the shot and more difficult the shot (rough, fairway bunker, etc.), the bigger your target range (landing area) should be

In other words, for pretty much all full-swing shots, chances are that you are not going to hit most of these shots close to the pin. Even a pro from 100-125 yards in the fairway only expects to get the ball around 20 feet from the pin on average. As a mid to high handicap golfer or even a high- to mid-single digit handicap golfer, you should naturally expect that your own margin for error based on your average distance from the pin will be considerably wider than that of a tour pro.

Therefore, the primary function of approach shots is actually not to fire at the pin and hit the ball within close range of the hole, since we have already seen that this is simply not what occurs most of the time. Nonetheless, taking dead aim and firing for pins on all approach shots is precisely what most struggling golfers do.

Instead, the primary function of approach shots to the green is also simply "positioning." This means that when facing an approach shot to the green, our primary objective should be to hit the ball in some proximity on or near the green that leaves us the easiest possible next shot. In other words, the goal of approach shots to the green is not to hit the ball close to the hole (although occasionally some shots will end up right by the hole), but to hit the ball in a position that will enable us to easily hit our next shot (be it a pitch, chip, or putt) close to the hole.

From a full-swing-shot distance to the green, we are not yet, or should not yet be, concerned with "getting the ball close" to the hole. Rather, we should first calculate our reasonable expected target range and margin for error based on our distance from the pin, the difficulty of the shot at hand, and our reasonable capability of executing the shot.

Next, having calculated our approximate target range, we need to survey the landing area. Are there bunkers or water or other hazards lurking within our chosen landing area? Might our target range leave us dangerously short sided, in a position where our next shot would be very difficult to hit close to the hole? If so, we may need to either expand our target range (margin for error) or shift our target further away from the hole. In some cases, we may conclude that our target area should even include an area off of the green, or in some cases, having weighed all of the factors of our shot, the target area may not even include the green at all, and instead be a bailout shot that steers us well away from round-killing trouble that lurks nearby.

We will discuss this decision-making process in more detail in the Course Strategy section of this book. For now, it is enough to realize that since it is not realistic to expect to hit the ball close to the hole with your full-swing approach shots to the green with any regularity, your primary target range (which should always be expanding and contracting depending upon the distance from the hole and overall difficulty of the shot) should usually be either the green itself, the green plus some relatively safe area around the green, or in some cases, simply a safe area near the green.

Similarly, your main priority with approach shots should simply be to ensure that you position yourself in such a way that your next shot is relatively easy while taking care to avoid the dangers that lurk nearby. In many cases this will mean that the pin itself is not included in your target area. Never be afraid to play away from the pin when the shot dictates that doing so is the most prudent play.

An easy way to remember our basic working philosophy for approach shots is:

Make Aggressive Swings to Conservative Targets

Based on this understanding of the function of drives and approach shots, let me now introduce to you what I call The New Rule of Target Golf, which you should adopt and employ in your own game in order to maximize your own ability to shoot lower scores:

The New Rule of Target Golf

The target for any shot should expand, contract and shift based on the distance from the hole and the overall difficulty of the shot

Allow this concept to jell as you read on.

Function of Short Game Shots

Now that we have defined the functions of drives and approach shots to the green, what about short game shots?

We have already seen that the function of the longer full swing shots that we face on the golf course is simply positioning, whereby our target range is relatively large and the shots do not require us to be highly precise in terms of accuracy. With our drives and full approach shots into the green, we are not trying to hit a target as small as the hole. Rather, our target range for these shots is actually quite wide, and usually offers plenty of margin for error.

As we get nearer the green, however, our target range begins to contract as we zone in closer to the hole. With our short game shots from just off the green or even little partial-swing wedge shots 20 or 30 yards off the green, the function of our shot changes from simple positioning.

The function of short game shots is to get the ball within our highly probably scoring or hole-out range

Notice that with full shots, our focus is not on trying to get the ball close to the hole, but rather, navigating around the hole and positioning ourselves in as advantageous a spot as possible while avoiding the troubles that lurk along the way.

We know from just a brief statistical analysis of the accuracy stats of the best players in the game, the PGA Tour pros, that consistently getting full shots to land in close proximity to the hole, never mind into the hole itself, is not a reasonable goal in most cases. Therefore, in hitting full shots we content ourselves with a relatively defensive strategy, expanding our target range as each shot requires, and simply focus on positioning ourselves to targets from which we can then begin to focus on the area of the game where true scoring takes place.

The short game shots are the shots from which we begin to focus on scoring. Short game guru Dave Pelz has estimated that short game shots account for as much as 80% of a player's handicap, and I am about to show you why I agree with this assertion.

We have already discussed how the vast majority of our hole-outs occur from short-putt distance range, a range of within 10 feet of the hole or so. Once we get outside of this range, the probability of our holing out the shot diminishes rapidly. Conversely, the closer we can get the ball to the hole within our scoring range, the higher probability we have of consistently holing the putt.

Therefore, based on what we know about the importance of getting the ball within our scoring range in order to have a great chance of holing out the shot, we can now understand that the function of short game shots—those shots just off the green or in near proximity to the green—is no longer mere positioning, but quite a bit more specific: to get the ball firmly within our scoring range.

Our statistical analysis tells us that even the very best players in the world cannot hit the ball consistently within our scoring range from longer distances.

However, if we look at the statistics of these golfers with regard to short game shots around the green, we can see that we have finally arrived at the distance in golf from which we most definitely can reasonably get the ball consistently within our highly probable hole-out range.

From 20-30 yards from the hole, a tour pro gets the ball up and down just over 50% of the time. This means that from this distance, 50% of the time they were able to hit the ball close enough in order to hole the next putt, and as we will see from our analysis of putting proficiency, this actually means that on average, the pro hits the ball to within just under 10 feet of the hole from this distance.

From 10-20 yards from the hole, a PGA tour pro is able to get the ball up and down around 65% of the time. The average proximity to the hole from this distance is to within about 7 feet.

As the PGA tour pro gets closer to the hole, the picture improves even more. From 10 yards and in, PGA tour pros, on average, get the ball up and down a whopping 85% of the time! Their average proximity to the hole from this range is just a little over 3 feet!

Can you begin to see the correlation between distance to the hole and the likelihood of consistently hitting the ball close enough to the hole to hole out the next shot? Can you begin to see the intimate connection between the short game and scoring? Can you see how as we get closer and closer to the hole, fulfilling the function of the shot has a greater impact on your ability to score, and conversely, how not fulfilling the function of the shot as you get closer to the hole will prevent you from realizing your maximum scoring potential?

Hopefully you can begin to see why it is vital that you begin to focus your attention on improving your short game, if indeed shooting lower scores and consistently breaking 80 is your goal.

In review, it is clear that the function of the short game shots, in other words, the task that we as golfers must accomplish with these shots, is to hit these shots within our highly probable hole-out range, and the closer and more straightforward our shot, the closer we need to hit the ball to the hole in order to ensure that we can hole out the next shot and save those all-important strokes that will enables us to improve our scoring and eventually gain the ability to break 80 consistently.

Function of Putts

What is interesting about putting is that the function of the putt depends upon the type of putt we are faced with. If you ask most high and mid handicap golfers what the function of a putt is, the majority would likely answer: hit the ball in the hole.

However, as we continue our brief statistical analysis, we will see a different sort of picture emerge. We will see that even once we get the ball on the green, we still may not be in true scoring range.

In fact, depending upon the distance we are from the hole (as well as the difficulty of the putt in terms of speed, slope and break), many putts actually fall into the same category as the short game shots we just looked at. That is, the function of longer and more difficult putts is the same as the function of short game shots: not to get the ball into the hole, but rather, simply to get the ball within very close proximity to the hole. With that in mind, let us take a look at each type of putt and its respective function.

Function of Long Putts (Lag Putts)

You may be surprised to learn that very few long putts ever find their way to the bottom of the cup. This is true for PGA Tour pros, and it is even truer for amateurs. In fact, from over 25 feet from the hole, tour pros, on average, 3-putt over 25 times over the course of a season and make barely 5% of their putts from this distance. As we get farther from the hole, we actually find that we have a greater likelihood of 3-putting than we do holing the putt.

Therefore, the function of a long putt is clear: lag it as close as possible to the hole without concern over actually holing the putt, and avoid 3-putting.

In terms of its function, a lag putt is much like a short game shot. We are trying to get the ball as close as possible to the hole within our scoring range, while not expecting to actually hole out the shot with any regularity.

Many high- and mid-handicap golfers and even single digit handicap golfers ignore the importance of lag putting, but they do so at the cost of valuable strokes added to their scorecard.

It is essential to understand the difference in terms of strokes saved by a golfer consistently able to lag his or her long putts to within 3 feet of the hole and a golfer whose lag putts usually finish 5-6 feet or even farther from the hole.

Lag putts can be deceptive. Instinctively the golfer knows he or she is unlikely to make the putt, while at the same time, is relatively confident of being able to roll the ball somewhere in the vicinity of the hole.

What most amateur golfers fail to realize is that when it comes to scoring, there is a massive difference between lagging the ball "somewhere in the vicinity of the hole" and developing the ability to consistently lag the ball to within imminent hole-out range.

Simple math bears this point out. If a golfer on average holes 50% of 5-footers and 90% of 3-footers, by only lagging the ball to within 5 feet of the ball verses 3 feet from the hole, the golfer is increasing the number of strokes he is likely to take for these shots, which occur with great frequency in every round of golf for players of all levels, by a factor of 40%.

Therefore, it is essential to understand the true function of lag putts, and to develop the ability to consistently lag long putts to within very close proximity of the hole in order to ensure maximum strokes saved.

Function of Medium-Range Putts

As we get closer to the hole, to a range from just outside of our True Scoring Range to just inside our lag putt range, which would be a range of about 10-25 feet, our prospects for holing putts from this range improve somewhat, but not as much as most golfers might believe. A glance at PGA putting stats will back up this assertion.

From a distance of 15-25 feet from the hole, PGA tour pros make on average just over 15% of their putts. Not bad, but clearly even the best players in the world miss the majority of putts from this distance range.

From a distance of 10-15 feet from the hole, the tour pros do much better, holing around 30% of their putts from this range. That is considerably better, but it still indicates that the best of the best still miss plenty more from this range than they make.

What these stats tell us is that when putting from medium-range distances, since we're still going to miss more putts than we make, we must approach these putts in such a way as to maximize our chances of making these putts while still ensuring that when we do miss, we leave the ball right near the hole so that we almost always hole out the next putt.

Indeed, from 10-15 feet from the hole, tour players on average 3-putt no more than 1% of the time. Even from 20-25 feet, tour pros 3-putt no more than about 2% of the time.

What this means is that for these medium-range putts, we want to focus on attempting to hole them, while being highly mindful of our distance control so that when we do miss, we have nothing more than a tap-in left to deal with.

Function of Short Putts

We now finally come to the shot in golf that is where scoring truly takes place. Notice that with every shot type we have analyzed so far, from drives to longer putts, the function of these shots has been to position ourselves increasingly closer to the hole, but not to actually hit the ball into the hole. Only when we get into short-putting range are we finally in position to have a high probability of holing out our shot and thus saving a stroke.

Our Theorem of Scoring tells us that the closer we are to the hole, the greater the relative impact of that shot on our score.

Indeed, with every positioning-type shot, we always have a reasonable margin for error. For instance, even when facing a 15 foot putt, although we may try to make it, we know that on average we will miss it more often than not, and when we do miss it, as long as our shot ends up within our target range for the function of the shot (in this case our target range might be within tap-in distance of the hole), it doesn't really matter if we miss it a bit to the left or to the right or short or long.

However, when it comes to short putting, our target contracts to an absolute target: the hole. Our objective also changes—from merely trying to position the ball in proximity to the hole, to actually hitting the ball in the hole. In other words, the function of short putting is clear: to hit the ball into the hole.

If we succeed in hitting the ball into the hole from short range putting distances, we have fulfilled the function of our shot and succeeded in saving a stroke. If we do not succeed in hitting the ball into the hole from our short range putting distance, there is only one end result: an extra shot added to our scorecard.

other position on the golf course is the impact of missing final. A short putt that we do not hole is a shot added to our riod. A short putt that misses by a fraction of an inch counts as much as a short putt that we miss 2 feet wide—one whole extra stroke.

It is only from short-putting range that our margin of error is reduced to the size of the hole. Therefore, when it comes to short putting, it is imperative that we understand the following:

1) Short putting range is the distance range from which the majority of all golf shots are actually holed

2) Short putting range is the distance from which we have a statistically reasonable expectation of holing our shots and thus saving a stroke

3) The sole function of short putting is to hit the ball in the hole; no other outcome is acceptable

From about 8 feet from the hole, we finally arrive at the distance from which most tour players expect, on average, to hole greater than 50% of their shots. From 6 feet away, the percentage of makes goes up significantly, to above 70%. From 5 feet, just one foot closer to the hole, pros hole out over 80% of their putts. From 4 feet, PGA pros hole their putts at over 90% proficiency. And from 3 feet, the shortest distance outside of virtual "gimmie" range, pros are almost automatic, at close to 99%!

So what do all of these numbers tell us? Actually, they provide us with some very compelling information. First of all, they suggest the upper limits of what is possible in terms of how precise we can expect to be with our short putting. Since PGA tour pros are the best golfers in the world who work diligently at their craft on a full-time basis, we know that it is unreasonable to expect that we can do better than they can. At the same time, the stats of the pros also suggest what we can possibly aspire to accomplish.

Our analysis of the various shot functions and accompanying stats also reveals two remarkably important pieces of information, which we must embrace and fully comprehend in order to ever hope to improve our ability to score and break 80 on a consistent basis:

1) **It is only from close range near the green and on the green that we can reasonably expect to hit a ball close to the hole (within our True Scoring Range)**

2) **It is only from within close proximity to the hole (our True Scoring Range, consisting of short putts) that we can reasonably expect to hit the ball into the hole**

Every shot that does not fall into one of the above two categories is merely a positioning shot, with a considerably large target range and relatively wide margin of error. As such, the impact of these positioning shots on our score is relatively small.

Conversely, every shot which does fall within one of the two categories above is a scoring shot with a much smaller target range and smaller margin for error. As such, the impact of these scoring shots on our score is relatively large.

The true key to scoring, therefore, is (once again):

1) **Hitting the ball into the True Scoring Range (short putt range)**

2) **Hitting the ball into hole (making short putts)**

The "One-Two" Scoring Punch

Indeed, this combination of short game shots (with which we can reasonably expect to hit the ball close to the hole) and short putts (with which we can reasonably expect to hit the ball into the hole) comprises our "one-two" scoring punch that will enable us to maximize our ability to shoot low scores, and ultimately, the ability to break 80 and shoot consistently in the 70s.

Just as a boxer's "one-two" combination is his fundamental bread and butter move he relies on and practices endlessly to defeat his opponent in the ring, our one-two golf scoring punch is the fundamental skill set that we must work on and refine in order to maximize our scoring potential on the course.

How is Your "One-Two" Scoring Punch?

Hopefully by this point you have grasped the significance of the short game and short putts, and now realize the importance of developing the ability to execute these shots at a proficient level if you ever hope to be able to shoot low scores in golf.

It is now time for a bit of self-assessment. How is your own "one-two" scoring punch? Are you able to execute these shots with anywhere near the proficiency of a pro?

Now at this point you may argue: I can't hit a 300-yard drive like a tour pro, so why should you expect me to be able to sink putts from 3 feet or hit greenside chips close to the hole with the same proficiency as a pro?

Indeed, the fact is that unless you invest the same amount of time working on your putting and short game as a pro does on his, chances are you will never quite reach that level.

Here is the big difference though: most amateur golfers can spend the rest of their lives trying and never hope to approach a pro's ability when it comes to ball striking. The good news, though, is that as it relates to the ability to break 80, this doesn't really matter. You don't have to become anywhere near as good a ball striker as a pro. You simply have to become good enough that you can fulfill the function of each shot, as we discussed earlier.

When it comes to the short game, however, the fact is that there is no physical impediment to being able to execute on a level that approaches that of the pros. An 80-year-old golfer has the ability to sink a 3-foot putt, or even hit a 30-foot chip close to the hole. In order to sink 3-foot putts at a very high level of proficiency, it isn't exceptional strength or speed or athleticism or even coordination that matters: it is simply precision and a bit of focused practice!

The same is true with most other short game shots on and right around the green (with a possible exception being greenside bunkers). You may not have the time or even the talent to actually match the ability of tour pros when it comes to the short game. However, there is no physical reason why any able-bodied golfer who invests a bit of effort cannot at least come reasonably close to doing so.

In other words, you may not have the time or inclination to practice your 3-foot putts to where you can sink 99% of them on average like a tour pro does. But are you willing to invest the time necessary to get to where you can hole out, say 80% of them? From 6 feet away, you may not be able to make 70% of your putts like the pros do, but can you put forth the effort to develop the ability to make 50% of them?

Likewise, you may not be able to get up and down from within 10 yards of the green 90% of the time like a pro does, but are you willing to practice to where you can at least do so over 50% of the time?

If you can reach even these levels, then you will have a very good chance at developing the ability to break 80 consistently, regardless of what your current level of skill is.

When it comes to scoring in golf, it all comes down to the short game. If you can develop a proficient short game, your scores can and will improve, in many cases dramatically. However, if you ignore your short game, you must understand that your scores are unlikely to improve significantly even if you spend a lifetime beating balls on the range and adopting the latest trendy swing theories.

Even if you do significantly improve your long game, eventually you'll reach a point where you hit a wall in terms of your ability to shoot lower scores, simply because almost all of the shots you are losing to par come as a result of failing to execute golf's "one-two" scoring punch at a sufficient level to shoot 80 or better.

Therefore, now that you know what really matters when it comes to scoring in golf, you now find yourself at a crossroads in your golfing life, with two clear choices:

1) Keep doing the same ineffective things you have been doing. Buy more new clubs, buy more new training aids, take more full swing lessons, keep beating balls, watch the Golf Channel and read Golf Digest in search of the magic cure all for your game, and continue to struggle and be frustrated, while never quite reaching your scoring potential.

Or:

2) Commit to the only known "shortcut" to lower scoring in golf: dedicate yourself to improving your putting and short game, refine your ability to manage your way around the course through better decision making (intelligent positioning) based on reasonable and statistically supported expectations for your results, and watch and enjoy as your scores literally drop off your scoreboard forever.

If you enjoy beating balls, swapping out your bag for new clubs every year, analyzing and dissecting your swing to the nth degree, then by all means keep doing those things, but do so with the understanding that you are not likely to improve your golf game significantly. Recall again Einstein's famous saying:

"Insanity is doing the same thing over and over and expecting different results"

If you truly want to improve your ability to score in golf, then realize that you need to start taking different action in order to achieve different results.

The 80-20 Principle

In business, there is principle known as the Pareto Principle, also known as the 80-20 rule, the law of the vital few.

In a nutshell, this principle states that for many events, roughly 80% of the effects come from 20% of the causes. Perhaps nowhere is this truer than as it pertains to scoring in golf.

As applied to golf, the application of the 80-20 Principle is clear:

When it comes to scoring in golf, 20% of our effort will be responsible for 80% of our scoring result. As we have already seen, that 20% of golfing effort that affects 80% of our score is the short game.

On a practical level what this means is that 80% of any scoring improvement we can ever hope to achieve will come from our effort at the short game. Even if we devote 80% of our time beating balls on the driving range while only spending 20% of our practice time on our short game, it is that 20% of practice time that will account for 80% of any scoring improvement we can reasonably expect to achieve.

Perfect Practice

We now return to the subject of practice. Despite the protestations of Allen Iverson, few people ever improve at a skill without diligently practicing that skill. Even if you're a person who prefers to play over repetitiously hitting balls on the range, you can certainly practice many aspects of your game on the course while you play.

Earlier in this book we debunked the myth that practice makes perfect. When it comes to golf, the truth is that practice makes permanent, not perfect. Since golf practice tends to involve extreme repetition, in the form of hitting golf ball after golf ball on the driving range, what we do through practice tends to evolve into deeply ingrained habits. If we end up practicing the wrong things the wrong way, then these wrong motions can quickly form into bad habits that can plague our progress, and in many cases, continue to do so over our entire golfing lifetime.

Bad habits can not only manifest as poor mechanical swing and stroke habits, but also as poor practice habits. An obvious example based on what we now know about the truth about scoring in golf is robotically beating balls on the range (and in doing so further ingraining bad swing habits), while either completely ignoring or paying scant attention to putting and the short game.

Perfect Practice for Breaking 80

We already know that insanity is doing the same thing over and over again and expecting different results. Based on what we now know about scoring in golf, if we want to truly improve our scores and achieve the ability to break 80 consistently, it is essential that we alter our approach to practice in such a way that improving our ability to score becomes our number one priority.

Going back to the 80-20 Principle, if we now know that 80% of our scoring improvement will come from the work we do on putting and the short game, is it not in our best interest to begin practicing in a way that will produce the results that we desire?

ROI

Another way to look at golf practice is in terms of your return on investment (ROI). In any endeavor, including golf, we make an investment of time, energy and money. We do so in the hope or expectation of achieving positive results. When we invest money in a stock or business venture, we hope or expect to earn a profit. When we invest time and energy in improving our golf game, we hope or expect real improvement that manifests in the form of lower scores.

However, just as any intelligent investor knows that it is not enough to simply blindly throw money at any bad investment, the intelligent golfer knows that it is not enough to simply beat balls on the range blindly with no structure or purpose and expect improvement. An investor who follows this approach and thoughtlessly throws money at bad investments may lose every bit of money he invested. Likewise, a golfer who follows this approach and thoughtlessly throws time and energy at bad practice habits can likewise expect to lose that time and energy with no tangible results, and possibly end up even worse than she was before.

Therefore, if you are going to make a commitment to invest your time and energy in practice for the purpose of improving your game and shooting lower scores, make sure to do so in a way that promises the greatest return on investment for your effort.

Perfect Practice for Maximum Improvement

So now that we know that practice makes permanent, and only perfect practice makes perfect, how should we approach our practice in order to maximize the return on our investment of time and energy (and money) in the form of better golf scores?

We simply design an approach to practice that is based on what we now know to be true about scoring and breaking 80. In case you've forgotten, allow me to refresh your memory:

The closer the shot is to the hole, the greater the positive impact fulfilling the function of that shot will have on your score

Now that we know that making or missing a 3-foot putt will have a greater impact on our score than splitting the fairway with our tee shot or hitting the ball into the rough, and now that we know that the ability to hit a 10-yard pitch shot to within 6 feet of the hole will have a greater impact on our score than will hitting the middle of the green from 150 yards away, we simply must begin to orient our practice in such a way that the majority of our time and effort is devoted to improving our proficiency at the short game.

New Paradigm for Golf Improvement

We know how the majority of the golfing population practices, and we know that it is not effective. We know that doing the same thing over and over again and expecting to achieve different results is a form of insanity. And we therefore know that if we want to achieve different (better) results, we need to approach golf in a different and better way.

In the old paradigm of golf improvement, we focused the bulk of our energy on improving our full swing and full-swing shot making ability. We sought the answers to our golf problems through swing changes, new equipment purchases, golf (swing) lessons, and video swing analysis, as well as through golf magazine "tips" and advice on Internet message boards.

In our new paradigm for golf improvement, we simply begin attacking our problem from the beginning at the source. We commit ourselves to a scoring-focused, target-based approach to practice.

Scoring-focused Approach to Golf Improvement

If you truly want to improve your ability to score at golf, then you must commit to working on those aspects of the game that most impact your score. This means putting and the short game, along with course management (on-course strategy) and developing and maintaining the proper mental/emotional approach.

What does this mean on a practical level? In broad terms it means that if you have an hour after work three times per week to practice in preparation for your weekend game, you spend all or at least the majority of that time working on your short game.

It means that instead of buying a large bucket of balls and heading to the driving range, you instead head over to the practice green. However, once you get there, you don't simply do as the majority of golfers practicing their putting do and mindlessly slap balls at the hole.

Rather, you devote yourself to an intelligently organized routine focused on developing your ability to sink more short putts, maximizing your opportunity to make medium-length putts while being conscious of distance control, and consistently being able to lag long putts within imminent hole-out range.

You commit to doing these things simply because you now know that doing these things is what is going to lead to better golf scores. You resist the temptation to rush out and beat balls because you now know that doing so will only further ingrain the fundamentally flawed swing habits you already possess. Therefore, when you do work on your swing, you spend more time at home in front of a full-length mirror working on your alignment and setup (aspects of the swing you have total control of and can monitor and can receive instant feedback on) and less time hitting balls on the range (action that is more difficult to monitor and receive instant feedback on unless you have a willing second pair of eyes or a video camera handy).

If you do choose to hit balls, you hit a small bucket rather than a large bucket, and you hit each shot with a purpose. You have a clearly defined target and shot shape in mind, and you visualize a situation on the course. You take your time aligning yourself and setting up, and you put thought behind your full-swing practice. And you DO NOT overdo it!

Instead, you make sure to spend ample time practicing your short game. You find an area where you can practice your little chip shots and pitch shots, and you invest the practice time learning how to get out of a bunker consistently.

You do all of these things because you now know that these are the things that are going to enable you to significantly improve your golf scores.

You diligently work on your putting and short game even while everyone around you continues to do the same thing over and over again, expecting different results. You smile to yourself because you know that you are now taking different, better action, and you are quickly starting to see the evidence that your investment is paying off in the form of lower golf scores.

Target-focused Approach to Play and Practice

As we have already discussed, the approach to golf of most golfers is highly swing focused. In order to truly maximize your ability to score in golf, it is essential that you become target focused rather than swing focused.

Earlier, I pointed out that in golf, the target for any given shot expands and contracts depending upon the length of the shot and difficulty of the shot at hand. A glance at the performance stats of PGA tour pros bears this out. Simply put: as a general rule, the farther one is from the hole, the greater the shot dispersion and therefore the larger the target must be, and conversely, the closer one is to the hole, the narrower the shot dispersion and the smaller the target must be.

If we apply this idea to actual golf shots we commonly face, it is easy to see how this notion is true. From tap-in distance, our target range, here meaning the range within which we can reasonably expect to hit the ball into the hole on an unfailing basis, is the hole itself. It continues to be the hole as we move back 3, 4, 5, and even 6 feet. From these distances, we still have a high expectation of hitting the ball into the hole much more often than not.

As we move even farther back, to 10, 15, and 20 feet, at some point our target range expands, and it becomes a target that is somewhat larger than the hole. From these distances, our target range may still include the hole, but actually be comprised of a circle about 2-3 feet in diameter surrounding the hole.

Once we are more than 30 feet or so away, our target expands even further, perhaps to a circle 3-4 feet in diameter surrounding the hole. In other words, provided we can consistently hit the ball within such a target from this distance range, we have fulfilled the function of the shot. Notice that by now, even while our expanding target range may still include the hole, from this distance we do not necessarily expect to actually hole a high percentage of shots from this distance.

Once we move off the green completely, our target will expand even further. Facing a little pitch shot of about 30 feet from a couple yards off the green, our reasonable target range may now be a circle surrounding the hole that is now 10 feet wide (which would leave us with a putt of 5 feet or less).

As we get even further from the hole and our reasonable target range continues to expand, the hole itself may no longer even be included within our target range. For example, from 75-100 yards away, even the average tour pro only hits the ball to within 17 feet from the hole or so. Knowing this, our target for this shot not only may expand to a circle about 40 feet in diameter, but depending upon the hazards that lurk nearby, our lie, our angle of approach, and other factors, it may become prudent for us to actually shift our target away from the hole to a wider open area on the green to the left or right of the hole (on-course strategy).

As we continue to move further and further away from the hole, so too does our target range continue to expand proportionally, to the extent that the entire green or a portion thereof, or even a portion of the green and an open area to the left or right of the green, may become our reasonable target.

For tee shots, our target may simply be a reasonable distance out into the fairway, or even in the rough but on the side of the hole that gives us the safest landing zone and best angle for our next shot.

Note that our target expands and contracts primarily based on the distance from the hole, but it also expands and contracts based on the difficulty of the shot. For example, if you find yourself faced with a pitch shot over a bunker to a hole only a couple paces off the green sloping away from you and with very little green to work with, even though from a pure distance perspective your target range may be, say, a circle surrounding the hole about 8 feet in diameter, because of the particular difficulties of this shot, you opt to expand and shift your target to a more reasonable distance (for example, a circle about 12 feet in diameter beyond the hole). By doing so, you eliminate any thoughts of attempting a heroic flop shot that you can only reasonably pull off perhaps 3/10 times, and instead opt for the simple pitch that leaves you about 8 feet away nearly every time, with still a reasonable chance to save par while taking double bogey out of the equation.

Likewise, pretend that you hit a decent drive that just dribbles into the rough about 150 yards from the hole. However, when you get to your ball, you find that you have a horrible lie. Normally your target for this shot might be the left half of the green, which includes the pin, but because of the unpredictable nature of the lie, you decide to shift and expand your target to the much more open right side of the green and even include an open area just off the green to the right, in order to avoid possibly pulling your ball into a creek that borders the left side. You alter your target, and indeed your shot sprays out and finishes a little short and right. However, by shifting and expanding your target you have left yourself plenty of green to work with and still have an excellent chance of getting the ball up and down for par, or at least make no worse than bogey.

The key principles of target-focused golf here are twofold:

1) **Become aware of the expanding and contracting nature of the target depending upon the length and difficulty of the shot at hand**

and

2) **Orient your play and your practice so that you focus on developing the ability to consistently hit your established targets, which are appropriately sized according to the type of shot you face**

Developing the Ability to Play Target Golf

How do we develop the ability to play target golf? First of all, we must learn to establish reasonable targets for each shot, expanding and contracting them as appropriate based on the challenge posed by each shot as well as our ability to execute the shot.

Although it is useful to reference the average target accuracy range of the pros from various distances (the STATS section of pgatour.com is an excellent source for this), and even to set such pro-level performance as an ultimate performance barometer for ourselves, the reality is that for mid and high handicap golfers still struggling to break 80 consistently, the actual target ranges for each distance and shot type, that is, the reasonably expected consistent shot dispersion, should be considerably wider than that of the pros.

That being said, however, in order to bring our ability to score to the point where we are shooting 80 or better, which is our working definition of "good golf" and the minimum level we aspire to play at, we must begin to train ourselves to hit target ranges within reasonable proximity to those of the pros, at least to the extent that doing so enables us to produce our working definition of Good Golf (the ability to shoot 80 or better).

Since we have established that there is a much greater physical and talent barrier for most golfers to hitting full shots as well as the pros, and since we have also established through our New Theorem of Golf Scoring that the closer the shot is to the hole, the greater the impact that shot has on the hole, if scoring improvement is our goal, then our wisest course of action is clear:

In order to maximize scoring improvement, the best course of action is to train ourselves to match or at least approximate the target-hitting proficiency of the pros, particularly at the close-range targets that present no true physical talent barriers, and which by doing so will have the greatest positive impact on our score

To put it in much more basic terms, this simply means: in order to maximize your scoring ability, it is essential that you commit to working on and improving your putting and short game.

The Problem with How We Learn to Play Golf

It has always been a mystery to me why, in almost every beginner's first golf lesson, the very first thing a novice is taught is the full swing. On the surface, perhaps this isn't so difficult to fathom. After all, in order to even get off the first tee and down the first fairway, we need to make a full swing at the ball.

Likewise, it is true that we cover the majority of the distance on the course with our full-swing shots. Please be clear that I am not denying the importance of learning how to develop a functional full swing that produces at least an adequate level of ball-striking ability.

However, I do question whether the conventional approach used almost universally by just about every golf teacher is the best approach that ultimately provides the golfer with the best opportunity to develop a fully well-rounded game, play good golf and shoot the lowest scores possible.

In my blunt opinion, this conventional lesson-tee approach is most definitely not the best approach. For starters, it is important to recognize that golf is a multidimensional game with many different skill sets that must be developed and mastered, at least to a reasonable proficiency level.

We have already established that the short game, that is, shots that require less than a full swing, accounts for well over half of the shots played in any given round of golf. We have also established that shots closer to the hole tend to have a greater impact on the score than shots farther away from the hole.

I would now like to suggest that even while shots closer to the hole have a greater impact on the score than shots farther away from the hole, shots closer to the hole are actually much easier to learn how to perform to a high degree of skill than shots further from the hole.

If you think about it, every shot in golf involves swinging a club back and through and hitting the ball toward a chosen target. Is it not easier for novice and less-accomplished golfers to learn to become proficient at shots with smaller, simpler swings at shorter distances, and then have their gained proficiency with smaller swings serve as the foundation for later success at becoming proficient with bigger, faster swings at longer distances?

The way golf is traditionally taught, a novice golfer will usually be asked to take a middle iron club, such as a 7-iron or a 5-iron. He or she will then be given basic instruction on the grip, stance, and swing, and then will be asked to step up and begin hitting shots.

Most novice golfers are unable to hit solid shots right away, even after having received basic instruction on how to do so, and so the inevitable first experience of nearly all beginning golfers is one of struggle, frustration, and failure. Right off the bat the new golfer develops a belief, based on her first experience with the game, that golf is extremely difficult.

Only a small handful of golfers are willing to gut it out through the early struggles and stick with the game for the long term. The sad reality is that most beginners' first impression of golf is that the game is just too hard, and so few actually stick with and commit to improving at the game.

Among those that do stick with the game, based on how they are initially taught to play and what they see other golfers doing, as well as what they read about the game in books, magazines, and on the Internet, etc., nearly all golfers conclude that the way to golf improvement is through beating balls on the driving range and developing a "perfect" swing through detailed analysis of the minute positions that occur during the swing.

I have already provided ample evidence showing the reality that most golfers simply do not improve with this approach. In fact, for many hardcore range rats, this approach usually only serves to reinforce the golfers' faulty swing habits through endless repetition, to the point where they become incapable of fixing their faulty swings even if they try.

As a result, it is not at all uncommon to see golfers who work on their golf games by routinely beating balls on the driving range practice for years, even decades, without ever significantly improving. Even if these golfers do succeed in building a semblance of a functional swing through their driving range practice, the majority of these range rats rarely if ever work on their short game, and so most invariably still struggle with the aspect of the game that most impacts their ability to shoot lower scores.

The most extreme example of this driving range mentality I can think of is an individual I encountered a few years back at my own local driving range.

This golfer was a man who started coming to the driving range where I practiced at regularly. He was a big man, probably in his mid-fifties or so. Having overheard him in conversation with other golfers, it was clear he was a very intelligent guy, who was earnest about improving his golf game.

One day I ended up hitting balls right next to him, and we began chatting. He told me that he was focused on improving his golf game, and that he had a plan: he was not going to even think about playing a round of golf until he developed the ability to hit his drives an average of 275 yards and with 80% fairway-hit accuracy.

I had some serious doubts about the wisdom of this approach. For one thing, I knew that not even one single tour pro had this capability. The perennial leader in driving accuracy, Joe Durant, averages around 75% of fairways hit. A middling tour pro hits just over 60% of his fairways, and many very successful tour pros barely even hit 50% of their fairways off the tee.

Nevertheless, since I knew that most golfers have strong attachments to their beliefs about their approach to the game, I bit my tongue and wished him good luck. Sure enough, over the next couple years I would see this man just about every time I visited the range, diligently working on his driver. He actually hit his driver quite well. He was a big guy with a decent swing, and he certainly was capable of hitting the ball 275 yards. He hit the ball pretty straight as well, easily well enough to take those drives out to the course.

Every now and then I would ask him how he was progressing. His stock reply was that he was coming along, but he still hadn't reached his established goals for the club, and so therefore he had not yet played a round of golf. Indeed, I noticed that even at the driving range, not only did he not ever even bring any club with him other than his driver, but he never once stepped foot on the putting green (of course, he wasn't the only golfer out there for whom that was the case!).

There were times when I wanted to ask the man whether even if he did succeed in hitting every drive perfectly, would he not be at a loss once he got anywhere near the hole, and I also wanted to suggest that it might be a good idea to practice his putting and short game as well as the other clubs in the bag once in a while.

Despite the fact that he actually developed into a very good driver of the ball, more than competent enough to step up on the first tee and begin hitting very respectable tee shots, somehow this rigid belief in his approach prevented him from even allowing himself to play a single round of golf. Eventually, he stopped coming to the range. Sometimes I wonder if he is still playing golf. Or perhaps I should say, I wonder if he has played his first round of golf yet...?

In the true story above, the man in question actually did develop the ability to hit some impressive full-swing shots with his driver, but even with his newfound driver progress, he still had the entire remaining golf skill set to tackle, not to mention a belief system that prevented him from playing a single round of golf even a full two years after first beginning to work on his game.

For the majority of golfers, the reality is that even if they were to adopt an approach like our hero in the story above, they would discover that even after years of practice, they still would not have developed a satisfactory level of ball striking.

In truth, many golfers who pursue ball-striking perfection on the driving range are not golfers in the true sense, and the game they are focused on—the game of "golf swing" or perhaps "ball strike"—is different from the game of golf played on the golf course, rather than on the driving range.

Indeed, there is a very large subset of golfers who are far more interested in developing the ability to hit pure golf shots off of a driving range mat than the ability to play the game of golf on the golf course.

Now, let me state for the record that as far as I'm concerned, there is nothing wrong with this approach, if that is in fact what you want to get out of the game of golf. Simply hitting balls on the range can be very pleasurable and rewarding, and there can be something very Zen-like about the single-minded pursuit of ball-striking perfection, where the faithful devotion to the ability to produce beautiful shots on the range is a means to its own end.

Golfers whose primary focus is ball-striking perfection through repetitive practice on the range should understand from the outset that what they are doing is most definitely not what a golfer ultimately needs to do in order to develop a fully well-rounded game and maximize one's scoring potential.

However, if developing the ability to shoot low scores and break 80 consistently is what you are most interested in achieving, you must grasp the fundamental truth that the game of scoring in golf is different from the game of "ball-strike" played on the driving range by many golfers.

At best, repetitively hitting full shots on the driving range covers only a small portion of the entire game of golf. At worst, it is a diversion of our attention away from those aspects of the game we most need to focus on in order to play better golf and shoot better scores.

Now, what if, in contrast to our driver-obsessed hero documented in the story above, we took the opposite approach and began developing our golf skill set from close proximity to the hole and progressing backwards?

What if instead of focusing on driver proficiency, our hero of the story proclaimed that he wasn't going to play a round of golf until he had pro-like proficiency on all of his putting and chipping and wedge play shots?

Now, you may begin to argue that the same thing that was true for the man in our story obsessed with mastering his driver will end up being true for us if we attempt to master our putter. What if we can't do it and end up doing nothing else but working on our putting for the next three years, while ignoring every other aspect of the game? How would we ever get off the first tee or make it on or near the green if we quit working on our swing and full-shot ball striking ability?

Well, I have a couple responses to these doubts. The first is that as golfers desiring to improve our ability to play the game and our ability to shoot lower scores, we need to adopt some type of intelligent approach to doing so.

Actually, most golfers, even those who practice earnestly at the game, have no real strategy for improving whatsoever. If they have any strategy at all, it consists of buying a large bucket of balls, and simply beating balls on the driving range without any rhyme or reason for doing so other than the fact that everyone else seems to be doing the same thing.

However, we have already established that when it comes to golf, practice makes permanent, not perfect, and therefore, if we want to improve our golf games, we need to practice in a precise manner, so that those things we practice which do inevitably become permanent, are practiced in such a way as to produce desirable, rather than undesirable, results.

Since beating balls on the driving range, at least without proper guidance, serves, for most golfers, only to further reinforce faulty swing habits, it is quite possible that the "beating balls on the driving range until your hands bleed" approach is not the optimal one for golf improvement.

Secondly, even while we work diligently at a particular area of the golf game in a focused, precise manner, this does not preclude us from still going out and playing. We can go out and play less-than-perfect rounds of golf while working intelligently at our game with a long-term improvement plan. The reality is that golf is a multidimensional game requiring a broad skill set, and that it takes a considerable long-term investment of time by all but the most naturally gifted of golfers in order to properly develop this full skill set.

Therefore, if we can accept the fact that developing a complete golf game will inevitably require time, patience, and diligent, precise practice, should we at least not approach our practice in such a manner that has the highest likelihood of yielding the positive results that we desire?

If you can agree with this logic, then the next step is once again clear. Commit to working on and improving those shots for which improvement and success is most reasonably attainable and for which improving will have the most immediate positive impact on scoring: putting and the short game!

Learning Golf "Backwards"

What if instead of the conventional "swing first" approach, we learned golf "backwards," at least from a conventional perspective? What if instead of attempting to first master the driver, and then the irons and the rest of the full shots, we instead focused on mastering the putter?

What if we first concentrated on learning to become proficient at holing out short putts, since we know that improving our ability to sink a higher percentage of these putts will improve our ability to score more immediately and with more certainty than anything else we can do for our golf game (based on our New Theorem of Scoring).

I'll be willing to bet that if, in the next month, you avoided hitting balls on the range and instead spent 2-3 hours per week doing nothing but working on your ability to make more putts from 3-6 feet, your golf scores will improve as a result.

Would you be willing to work on sinking 3-foot putts until you are able to consistently make 80% of them? Would you be willing to work on your 4-foot putts until you can make 70% of those? How about 60% of your 5 footers and 50% of your 6 footers?

Do you think that if you committed to working on nothing else than achieving the above performance levels for short putting, that your golf scores would improve as a result? I'll bet that unless you're in a very small minority of golfers who are gifted putters, if you are a high to mid-handicap or even high single-digit golfer you are not putting at that level just yet. And if you're not, then you are needlessly leaving many strokes out on the golf course!

The point I'm trying to make is that if you put in even a small bit of focused effort over the next golf season, or even the next month or so, improving your ability to make short putts, you will actually find that it is almost impossible to not improve significantly at this skill, and this improvement will instantly be reflected on your scorecard to the tune of lower golf scores.

Conversely, I'll bet that if you spent that same amount of time and effort doing nothing but hitting your driver on the driving range, even if you do succeed in improving your driving somewhat, you may be surprised to find that your scores do not necessarily improve much as a result. However, the more probable outcome is that even if you spend the next three months working on your driver, for the reasons we have already discussed (practice makes permanent) you are more likely to simply further ingrain your bad habits than you are to improve significantly.

Therefore, why not change the way you approach your golf improvement, and begin with improving the area of the game, short putting, that not only offers the highest probability that you will actually improve at that skill as a result of working at it, but which will also provide you with the greatest return on your investment of time and effort in the form of tangible improvement reflected on your scorecard.

Orienting your golf improvement plan based on this "learn golf backwards" approach has one additional and very important advantage. Since the putting stroke in general and short putting in particular is not a difficult movement, unlike the full swing, which is a relatively complicated movement, you will not need to focus so much on the nuances of your stroke and can instead focus on your target.

This approach will get you in the habit of becoming a target-focused golfer. By first committing to working on your short putting, you will be focused on the smallest, most precise target in golf: the hole. With a little practice you will train yourself to be completely focused on the task of hitting your target and sinking putts. And your scores will improve as a result.

Once you have become proficient at sinking short putts, now it is time to move back and become equally proficient at medium-range putts. Now that you understand the principle of target golf, you know that as you move further from the hole, the target expands. Therefore, from a distance of about 10-25 feet or so, you focus on being able to consistently hit the ball within a 2-3 foot circle. You know that if you work on consistently being able to accomplish this task, you will make your fair share of these putts, but you will as importantly begin to eliminate those round-killing 3-putts.

You'll find, after having worked diligently at your short putting proficiency, that it is not difficult at all to accomplish the above task. And you'll find that your scores begin to improve even more as a result.

Hopefully by now you are fully convinced of the effectiveness of this "backwards" approach to practice, and are now excited to begin working on your lag putting. You know that this overlooked aspect of putting is responsible for many 3-putts, which means many extra strokes on your scorecard. So you begin working on your ability to lag those long putts from 30-50 feet away right up to within 4 or more ideally within 3 feet of the hole.

You find that having developed your medium-length putting skill, that it is not too much of a leap to become proficient at consistently lagging your putts to within your high-percentage short-putt range. And since you have already put in the work with your short putting (and continue to work on and maintain this skill), once you do lag your long putts into your high-conversion short-putt range, you know that your lagging ability along with your short-putt-making ability combines to form your potent "one-two scoring punch" that continues to knock even more strokes off your scorecard.

I'll be willing to bet that if you spent the next couple months following the above program and do nothing else but commit to improving your putting, by the end of that time you'll be shooting significantly lower golf scores than you currently are today, and certainly, lower scores than you would be shooting if you continued to beat balls on the range like a robot.

I'll bet that if you are struggling to break 100 and you followed the above program, that you'll find yourself getting very close to or actually breaking 100 and begin shooting scores in the 90s. If you are stuck in the 90s, I'll be that after following the above program you'll find yourself getting your scores down into the 80s. And if you are an 80s golfer, I'll bet that just following the above program alone may be enough to get you knocking on the door of breaking 80, and may even get you over the hump into the magical land of shooting in the 70s!

Following our target focused "learn golf backwards" approach, let's see how we've progressed so far. Let's assume that we spent the last 2-3 months doing nothing else but working on our short game in the manner described above. Do you think that if you did this, that your scores would improve significantly as a result, and that you would be enjoying the game more than you are today?

Now, let's pretend instead that we did not work on our games using the "learn golf backwards" approach, and instead continued to go out to the driving range and hit bucket after bucket of balls. How do you think this approach would have worked for you in terms of improving your golf game? Since this is likely the approach you have followed so far in your golfing lifetime, with minimal improvement at best, the answer is pretty simple. I'd be willing to bet that if you do not follow this approach and instead commit all of your available practice time to hitting full shots on the driving range, that your scores will not improve significantly, or even at all, as a result.

Which of the two approaches above do you think would result in greater improvement? Do you think you're likely to improve more by hitting ball after ball on the driving range, when you know that practice makes permanent, and that repetitive beating of balls is only likely to further reinforce your existing swing flaws? Or do you think that by following an organized, target-focused and scoring-focused approach, working on skill sets with which you have a high likelihood for improvement, and which will provide you with the highest ROI in terms of actual improvement, will provide a better result?

Hopefully you are starting to become convinced of the wisdom of the "learn golf backwards" approach. Now, at this point you may start to argue: You want me to completely give up hitting golf balls? I can't completely neglect my long game!

Don't worry. You do not have to completely neglect your long game. You do not have to give up hitting golf balls cold turkey. However, why not follow the 80-20 Principle and shift your focus and energy on improving those aspects of golf that are going to clearly provide you with the greatest ROI?

Effective Full Swing Practice

I would even go to the extreme and say that you are likely to experience no adverse effects even if you were to give up hitting balls on the range completely. When you do work on your full swing, I would recommend that you spend the majority of your full-swing practice time at home in front of a full-length mirror. Work on your grip. Work on your set up. Work on your alignment. Just a few minutes per day working on these vital aspects of your game will pay huge dividends, as proper grip, setup and alignment are paramount for a fundamentally sound swing.

Make swings in front of a mirror. This will provide you with instant feedback, so that you can actually see what is going on in your swing while you swing. This mirror practice will also help you to equate the "feel" of your swing with the "real" of what is actually happening. This instant visual feedback of what is going on in your swing will allow you to focus on your swing mechanics without the distraction of having to hitting a shot. If you work on your swing in this way, you'll find that you will actually improve your swing and improve your ball striking much more than if you simply beat balls blindly on the driving range.

If you must hit balls, never hit more than a small bucket in one session (30 balls or so). Focus on each shot. Use an alignment aid and align yourself and set up carefully on each shot. Apply what you have learned from your target-oriented approach to the short game and make sure you have a specific target that is appropriate for each shot. Most importantly, recognize that it is very easy to fall back into old, ineffective habits. Therefore, avoid the almost irresistible lure of the practice tee that somehow possesses some mysterious magnetic force that almost seems to compel golfers to become ball-beating robots.

Avoid the temptation to hit "just one more bucket" even when you're not swinging well. In fact, you're better off hitting more shots when you are swinging well and cutting short those sessions when things are not going well. Often, simply regrouping and coming back the next day is all you need when you are off form.

Confine your full-swing sessions to the day before you go play, or as a warm-up to your round, but NEVER at the expense of working on your short game. Always put in your short game work first. Then, with whatever time you have left over, go ahead and work on your full swing shots.

Admittedly, it takes a certain amount of discipline to follow this "learn golf backwards" approach. After all, by doing so you will be taking the Road Less Traveled and swimming against the current. You'll be working diligently on your putting while everyone else is hitting ball after ball on the driving range. Even on the putting green, you'll be practicing in a focused manner while everyone around you is simply slapping putts haphazardly at the hole without purpose or plan.

However, the most fundamental Key to Breaking 80 is that the short game is where the scoring in golf takes place, and that if you want to enter the rarified realm of breaking 80 and experience the joy of shooting in the 70s, time and time again, then there is simply no way around it: you must work on and improve your short game.

Most Likely to Succeed

Let's examine the following two hypothetical scenarios.

Scenario 1:

You are introducing a new golfer to the game of golf. This novice golfer is excited to learn to play the game but nervous with anticipation because everyone has told her how difficult golf is. You take her to the driving range, put a 7-iron in her hands, and give her some basic instructions on how to grip and swing the club, and then give her a bucket of balls to hit. Predictably, even though your swing instruction may have been spot on, she struggles to hit solid shots, and her first impression of golf is that it is an impossibly difficult game.

Scenario 2:

You introduce your same novice golfer friend to the game of golf. However, instead of the driving range, you head on over to the practice green. You give her some basic instructions on how to grip and stroke the club. Then you set her up near a relatively flat hole and you instruct her to hit putts "around the clock" about 2 feet from the hole. She finds that she can accomplish this task fairly easily, and enjoys the pleasurable sensation of knocking in putts and hearing the beautiful plink of the putts landing at the bottom of the hole. Next, you move her back to about 3 feet from the cup. This she finds a bit more challenging. However, with a bit of practice she gets a feel for the speed and the various slight breaks, and after a while she is able to make the majority of her putts. Her first impression of golf is one of joy, excitement, positive reinforcement and success.

Now let's pretend that we continue with our instruction of our novice golfer. In Scenario 1, after she has swung a 7-iron for a while, you tell her it's time to try to hit a driver. Predictably, she struggles even more with this club.

In Scenario 2, after she has gotten the knack for holing 3-foot putts, you move her back to about 10-15 feet from the hole and challenge her to roll putts to within a 3-foot circle. This she finds challenging and difficult to do at first, but with a little practice, she begins to get this down as well.

A couple of hours have passed and so you call it a day. As you drive home, your novice golfer friend talks about her impressions of the game that she has experienced for the first time. How do you think her impressions of the game will differ in each scenario?

In Scenario 1, her experience has mainly been one of failure and frustration. Perhaps she hit a few decent shots, and that small success will be enough to bring her back for another day. But she is just as likely to conclude that golf too difficult, not worth the time, and decide that golf is not for her.

In Scenario 2, her experience has mainly been one of success. She was able to accomplish the tasks you set forth for her. She experienced success at holing putts, and this has given her confidence. She can't wait to come back and try some longer putts and even some chip shots from just off the green, which you promised to teach her the next time. She is definitely eager to come back for more.

The point of this little hypothetical scenario is simply to illustrate the difference in experience based on the two very different ways of approaching the game. Interestingly, this difference in experience tends to be similar even for much more seasoned golfers.

The fact is that if you are a struggling high to mid handicap golfer, most likely your predominant experience in golf is one of frustration and even failure. You struggle to swing, you struggle to hit solid golf shots, and you definitely struggle to score, even despite the fact that you work diligently to improve. This constant battle with frustration inevitably takes its toll on the psyche and self-confidence of even the most positive-minded golfers.

However, if you approach the game in such a way that enables you to begin experiencing success, then each small success, in the form of each holed putt you make or each progressively expanding target area you hit, will reinforce your growing self-confidence in yourself and your game.

You will find that if you follow this target-focused "learn golf backwards" approach, each small success will build progressively upon one another as you move further and further from the hole and gradually off the green, from very small strokes and swings made putting and chipping to progressively larger swings made pitching and hitting little wedge shots.

Once you follow this approach and get to the point where you are now making full swings, you will find that all the practice you did beforehand with the shorter shots in golf will serve as your solid foundation for success with your longer shots. Your experience of golf will be completely different, and ironically, it is not you or even your innate ability that will have changed, but rather, your approach to the game that has changed and finally enabled you to play better golf and shoot lower scores.

Why not therefore approach your golf game in a way that will enable you to experience success from the outset, in a way that will build your confidence and provide you with a solid foundation for a solid golf game, not to mention in a way that will enable you to maximize your scoring potential?

The Holy Grail of Golf

Undoubtedly, for many golfers reading this right now, the notion of abandoning your efforts to master the golf swing and instead devote the majority of your time to working on your short game and building a foundation for your game from the hole backwards is quite radical.

Even if you can grasp and accept the logic of this approach, the lure of the practice tee and pursuit of swing and ball striking perfection can be very strong indeed. There is something innately powerful about the desire to achieve swing mastery.

There is a type of golfer at the driving range I have practiced at for much of the past decade that can undoubtedly be found at every driving range around the world. This golfer is typically not interested in actually playing the real game of golf but rather, is obsessed with the pursuit of the Holy Grail of swing perfection.

This golfer comes to the range almost daily. He usually buys a large bucket of balls each session, sometimes two or more, and loses himself in the pursuit of ball striking perfection. Day after day, year after year, this golfer plugs away, hitting ball after ball, in hope that one day he will eventually find that "magic move," that Holy Grail that will enable him to hit perfect shots forever.

It is interesting to observe that this type of golfer hits balls endlessly on the range, but seldom if ever actually plays a round. It is also interesting to observe that this type of golfer will typically spend 2-3 hours working on his swing, but never once step foot on the putting green.

Perhaps this golfer plans to start practicing his putting and actually play rounds of golf after he discovers the Holy Grail of swing perfection. Maybe actually playing golf is of little interest to him. However, in either case, one thing is clear:

Swing Mastery is Elusive

Even the greatest golfer of our generation, Tiger Woods, clearly has a touch of the Holy Grail syndrome. Here is a golfer who is perhaps the most talented golfer who has ever played the game, who burst onto the PGA tour and literally steamrolled his opponents and lapped the field at majors and racked up tournament victories like a child collecting seashells on the beach.

And yet, dissatisfied with the perceived flaws in his swing, over the course of his career he has set about overhauling his swing not once, not twice, but three times. During each rebuild, he suffered through considerable stretches where his performance was relatively poor and he won far less. It is true that at least over the course of his first two swing rebuilds he was able to gain enough mastery over his swing that he was able to again win in prodigious fashion.

However, Tiger has been quoted as saying that each of his swing overhauls took about two years to complete. With three overhauls, that is six entire years of his golf career that he sacrificed for the sake of swing perfection which, even for Tiger, has continued to be proven elusive. One can only wonder how many more majors Tiger might have won so far if he simply stuck with what was working so well to begin with.

Ironically, Tiger Woods has clearly played his best golf and won the most when he has been able to shift his focus away from swing mechanics and on the creative process of shaping shots and hitting targets. Even as he struggled with his swing changes, he still was able to win with relatively poor ball striking thanks to his amazing short game and most importantly, his ability to sink those critical short putts at critical moments while his opponents did not.

The point of this slight digression is that if swing mastery is elusive even for Tiger Woods, perhaps the most talented golfer ever to play the game, who has all of the time and money and coaching and resources in the world available to him, is it not clear that swing mastery is even more unattainable for the golfer of average talent with limited time and resources?

If what you really want out of the game of golf is to simply enjoy the meditative pleasure of hitting balls on the range, and if the process of pursuing swing mastery is more appealing than actually learning how to play the game of golf, then by all means continue down that path.

Many golfers simply enjoy the sensation of hitting shots and enjoy the endless challenge of refining their swings and shot making ability. Much like a Zen archer, the joy is in the practice itself. Honestly, there is nothing wrong with this approach to the game. At various times of my own golfing lifetime I have fallen into this mode, and I too was perfectly happy with nothing more than to truly enjoy the sensation and the challenge and the pleasure of hitting shot after shot on the range.

However, if this is the golfing path you choose, it is important to recognize that this form of golf challenge is completely different from the challenge of actually playing the game of golf on a golf course, and that the ultimate purpose of this approach is not to maximize your ability to score, but rather, to enjoy the pursuit of the Holy Grail even while understanding that this pursuit is elusive at best and impossible at worst.

If, on the other hand, what you want out of golf is to be able to go out on the golf course and shoot the lowest scores possible and build a complete golf game, then it is time for you to consider a better, more effective approach designed to accomplish just this task.

Avoiding Injury

There is another compelling reason to avoid falling into the habit of becoming a robotic, ball-beating range rat: the prospect of injury. Most PGA Tour pros, as well as many recreational golfers, suffer from a host of golf-related chronic back, shoulder, hip, neck, and wrist ailments. What is worth noting is that in most cases, these injuries originate not on the course during play but on the driving range during practice.

Indeed, it is the repetitive stress of performing the golf swing, an unnatural motion that the body was not really designed for, over and over again on the practice tee that is the cause of an epidemic of physical ailments suffered by golfers.

What is the best way to avoid these repetitive stress injuries? Don't over practice, particularly with regard to the full swing! Although one must also be careful to not over-practice short game shots, as these too normally involve bending the body over in such a way that injury may occur over time, the full swing, in contrast, is a violent, one-sided motion which, when performed over and over again, may easily result in a host of physical pains.

Therefore, in order to avoid golf-related injuries, be sure to follow these guidelines.

▶ Make sure to sufficiently stretch and loosen up before any practice session or play

▶ Don't hit too many full swing shots in a single session. Focus on quality over quantity. Since the golf swing is such a one-sided motion, counterbalance this one-sidedness by routinely making swings to the other side (left-handed swings for right-handed golfers)

▶ Even when practicing short game shots, make sure not to stay bent over for excessive periods of time. Take periodic breaks and stretch

▶ Consider a golf-oriented exercise and fitness program to compliment your golf practice

The above are just a few cautions you should follow. Above all, practice common sense and remember that when it comes to golf, practice doesn't make perfect; only perfect practice makes perfect. Quality over quantity always!

Why Short Game Mastery is Highly Possible

While swing mastery is elusive even for the very best players in the game, short game mastery, or at least achievement of short game proficiency at a very high level, is well within the realm of possibility for any golfer of even modest natural talent who diligently applies oneself.

Many golfers spend years, decades even, in pursuit of swing mastery with no discernible results. In many cases, such golfers actually get worse over time. Very few golfers who pursue swing mastery ever achieve it, and most golfers who approach golf in this manner never make meaningful improvement in their ability to score.

In contrast, golfers who dedicate themselves to mastery of the short game, putting in a reasonable effort at developing the ability to play the various shots on and around the green, will invariably find that they make tangible, visible progress that is instantly reflected to the tune of better scores.

The reasons for this we have already touched on:

1) The swing is a difficult move to master, and most people who attempt to do so, without proper guidance and persistence, invariably end up only further ingraining poor swing habits.

2) Even if a degree of swing mastery is achieved, this still leaves more than half of all of the shots to be played in a round of golf that do not require a full swing.

3) The further away from the hole, the less precision is required and the smaller direct impact on the score. So, for instance, a 260 yard drive down the middle of the fairway instead of a 245 yard drive in the right rough will certainly help position the golfer better for his next shot. But it will not guarantee the scoring outcome of the hole and only marginally impact the player's score on the hole.

4) The closer to the hole, the more precision is required and the greater the direct impact on the score. Thus, the ability to chip the ball from just off the green to a circle surrounding the hole 8 feet wide as opposed to a circle 16 feet wide will directly result in more subsequent putts made, and thus, better scoring.

The difference between the pursuit of swing mastery and the pursuit of short game mastery is that the latter, short game mastery, is highly attainable for anyone who puts forth the effort, while swing mastery is highly elusive even for the most dedicated individuals.

Therefore, given the highly attainable nature of short game mastery versus full swing mastery coupled with the fact that short game improvement is more directly reflected on a golfer's scoring ability versus full-swing improvement, a golfer whose main objective is to improve and shoot lower golf scores would be well advised to focus on short game mastery rather than swing mastery.

Why is short game mastery highly attainable relative to the pursuit of swing mastery? Well mainly, because for able-bodied golfers there is no physical barrier to developing the short game to a high degree. A 3-foot putt involves swinging a putter with a simple back and forth motion using a stroke that covers perhaps two feet of ground. Everyone from a 5-year-old to a 90-year-old can perform this motion, and learn to do so capably and relatively quickly.

Likewise, a little chip from just off the green involves a bit more technique, but only a little bit more. This too is actually a very small and simple motion that any able-bodied golfer can learn to do with just a bit of practice.

Of course the challenge of putting and chipping involves not just the actual stroke, but the ability to read greens and judge distance. However, these are things that can be learned in fairly short order through experience with even a modest amount of focused effort.

In contrast, there is no getting around the fact that the full swing is very difficult for most golfers to gain even basic competency with, never mind true mastery.

Short Game Mastery as a Foundation for Longer Shot Mastery

There is another compelling reason why it makes sense for a golfer to develop his or her game from the hole backwards. Mastery of each shorter shot and shorter stroke ends up providing a solid foundation for learning and mastering progressively larger strokes.

A short putt stroke, and the ability to fulfill the function of short putts, will serve as the foundation for the physical motion and ability to fulfill the function of medium-length putts. The motion and function of long lag putts will serve as the foundation for the golfer's ability to perform a chipping motion and fulfill the function of that shot, and so on.

Once a golfer has gained competency at hitting partial wedge shots, say from a distance of 50 yards or so, he or she will find that this competency will serve as the foundation for the beginnings of the full swing.

Having focused on and gained competency at the entire range of shots up to partial wedge shots, it is no longer a great leap to translate this competency into a capable full swing with a wedge.

The golfer who has gained competency to hit partial wedge shots from 50 to 75 yards will find it not much more difficult to hit 100 yard full wedge shots to a slightly more expanded target. From here, it is only a matter of simple progression for the golfer to be able to achieve similar competency from all remaining distances and expanding targets.

So as you can see, the point of the "short game first" approach is not to ignore the long game, but rather, to build a true foundation that will enable the golfer to actually gain long game, full-swing, target-hitting competency once that stage of development is reached.

Shot-focused Golf

Another advantage of the "learn golf backwards" method is that this will orient you to becoming a shot-focused golfer rather than a swing-focused golfer. What does this mean in practical terms?

Most golfers may start out with the intention of being shot-focused golfers. They may be on the driving range with driver in hand, and have a target or even a shot shape in mind. However, they soon find it difficult to perform the shot they had in mind, and begin analyzing the nuances in their swings in order to find the "problem" that is hindering them from being able to pull off their desired shot and hit their intended target.

This shot, miss, and swing analysis pattern soon becomes habitual, to the point where the golfer's focus shifts from creating and executing shots to defined targets, to becoming preoccupied with the nuances of the swing.

The problem here lies in the original difficulty, for most golfers, in performing full swing shots. Full swing shots are relatively hard to perform, and most golfers cannot help but to look inward at their swings in hopes of diagnosing and solving the "problem" that will enable them to hit the shots they desire.

However, the real problem is not with the swing itself, but rather, the golfer's approach to developing his shot making skills. By beginning with attempting to perform the most complicated move in golf, the full swing, most golfers are setting themselves up for failure from the outset.

If, however, you were to adopt a "learn golf backwards" approach and begin developing your game from very close to the hole and progressively outward, you would find that the initial swings you need to make to perform these shots are relatively simple compared to the full swing.

This relative simplicity of movement will enable you to focus primarily on creating and performing the shot and hitting your chosen target, which in turn will get you in the habit of becoming a shot-focused golfer rather than a swing focused golfer.

Moreover, you will find that as you progress in developing your shot making ability, the shots you developed closer to the hole, and the swings required to perform them, will serve as the rock solid foundation for shots farther from the hole and the progressively larger swings required to execute them.

This will be true as you develop your short putting skills, which will serve as the foundation for your medium and long putting skills, which will serve as the foundation for your chipping skills, which will serve as the foundation for your pitching skills, which will serve as the foundation for your wedge game skills, which, will serve as the foundation for your short iron skills, your medium iron skills, your long iron/hybrid skills, your fairway wood skills, and finally, your driver skills.

Most importantly, by working on developing your ability to perform shots from closer to the hole to progressively farther away from the hole, you will not only develop your shot making ability for all shots, but you will do so without the need to focus on the nuances of the swing.

All accomplished golfers are shot-focused golfers, and if you want to develop the ability to play accomplished golf and break 80 on a consistent basis, you must become one too. The best way to do so is by developing your game in such a way that facilitates this approach and naturally develops the right golf habits that will enable you to play your best golf.

Course Management: How to Think Your Way to Lower Scores

On-course strategy, or course management, is closely related to target-focused golf. It is the seldom-discussed art of thinking your way intelligently around a golf course. Course management is the decision-making aspect of golf, which can have a deceptively powerful impact on your scorecard. Most struggling golfers are unaware of the potential strokes that can be saved simply by making better decisions on the golf course during the course of their round.

Beyond a vague idea of the direction they are aiming, most high-handicap golfers simply have no plan for a given shot, let alone the hole or the round as a whole. Standing on the first tee, driver in hand, most golfers simply aim down the middle and let it rip with little or no consideration of the following factors:

▶ The shape of the hole

▶ The hazards that lurk near the intended landing area

▶ One's own general ball flight tendency
   (hook, slice, draw, fade, etc.)

▶ One's own ball flight tendency for that particular day

▶ The wind direction

▶ The shot's safe landing zone

▶ The shot's danger landing zone

▶ An idea of what angle to ideally approach the next shot from

▶ A realistic target zone one can reasonably expect the shot to land within

These are just some of the factors that must be considered on every shot, which can and should influence your decision of what type of shot to play. For example, let's say that the hole is a sharp dogleg right with a bunker near the corner of the dogleg at your landing zone distance and your general shot driver shape is a fade-slice but there's a relatively safe landing area on the left side of the fairway, although there is a small pond pretty far out on the left, and there is also a pretty strong right-to-left wind. How would these factors influence how you plan to play your drive?

Well, first of all, we have some choices. We could try to play our fade-slice and cut the corner of the dogleg, if we have enough distance to do so, but we need to be aware that if we over cut it, our ball could land in the bunker or in the trees with no angle to the green.

Since we have a strong wind working against our natural shot shape, we can instead opt to aim down the left rough line and attempt to cut our drive back to the middle-left side of the fairway, which would leave us the best angle to hit our approach shot. Since we have the length to reach the pond with our driver if we end up pulling the ball left, which we do on occasion, we could instead hit a 3-wood to ensure that we land short of all of the trouble.

The shot we ultimately choose should weigh all of the above factors with the goal of settling on a shot that gives us the highest likelihood of succeeding, but which also has the highest likelihood of keeping us out of trouble in the event that we do not execute the shot exactly as we planned.

This is just one example of the type of thought process you should exercise before each and every shot. Now, this may seem like a lot of information to process. But once you get used to doing it, going through this type of decision making process really only takes a few seconds. Moreover, you can make a lot of your decisions as you approach each shot, or even before the round by planning out how you ideally want to play each hole, provided you are familiar with the course.

PGA Tour pros do this all the time. In fact, if you ever get a chance, go watch one of the practice rounds at a PGA Tour event. You may be surprised to see that during these practice rounds, the pros don't simply play a straightforward round of golf. Instead, they hit various shots from various angles, processing information, charting the breaks of greens and taking detailed notes in order to figure out the best way to play each hole come tournament time.

Now, we common golfers usually don't have the luxury to practice like that on the course, but we certainly can draw on our previous experience at courses we frequently play to learn what spots on each hole are advantageous and which spots to avoid like the plague.

For example, one course I play frequently is the North Course at Torrey Pines in San Diego. Although I've never had a chance to practice hitting shots on the course in the manner described above like the tour pros before an event, I have played the course enough times that I have learned where to hit the ball and where not to hit it.

For example, I know that on the first hole, a relatively easy par 5, there is room to miss left but a miss to the right leaves a difficult angle. I know that the rough is wide open on the right for the second shot, so even if I miss there I'll have a clean look at the green with my third shot. I know that it is very hard to get up and down from the back of the green, so I err toward taking less club for my approach shot.

Over the years I have also picked up on some general tendencies for that course. I know that almost every green on that course slopes considerably from back to front, and that the greens can be very quick from above the hole, so when playing this particular course I tend to err toward leaving the ball short and below the hole rather than long and above the hole. I also know that the nearby ocean can influence the break of many of the putts, and that I need to account for the strong wind that blows from off the Pacific Ocean.

You can pick up similar observations of your own home course and use them to your advantage to help you to shoot lower scores.

Even when you are playing an unfamiliar course, you must rely on your eyes to quickly figure out a shot-making plan for each hole and each shot. There are, however, some very general on-course strategy rules that you can apply to any course, and diligently following these rules will help you to maximize your scoring potential for each round of golf that you play.

- ▶ Play to your basic shot shape and don't try to "fix" your swing during a round

- ▶ Off the tee, play to the open side of the fairway and away from hazards

- ▶ Consider hitting a 3-wood or hybrid or even an iron off the tee if hazards lurk in your driver landing area

- ▶ Play to the fat part of the green and away from hazards

- ▶ Play your approach shots away from a tucked pin in order to avoid "short-siding" yourself

- ▶ Try to keep the ball below the hole in order to leave easier chips and putts

- ▶ If you get into trouble, your first priority is to get out of trouble, even if it means pitching back into the fairway or bailing out to the middle of the green

- ▶ Always think ahead while on the tee of the ideal angle you would like to approach your next shot from, and plan your shot accordingly while taking into account the hazards that lurk nearby

The above are just a few of the general strategy rules you can follow on any course in order to maximize your likelihood of shooting a good score.

Conservative Golf for Better Scores

Most high and mid handicap golfers would be better served by adopting a much more conservative approach to their game. The best way to describe this approach would be to say:

Hit aggressive, committed shots to conservative targets

Simply put, most struggling golfers do not leave themselves enough margin for error on their shots. On drives, since the shot dispersion of most golfers off the tee with a driver can be as wide as 30-50 yards, your focus should be simply to put the ball in play by hitting away from whatever trouble lurks off the tee. It's usually still fine if your ball lands in the rough, as long as you still have a shot at the green and you avoid the major trouble.

On approach shots to the green, most struggling golfers fire blindly at the pin without considering the consequences of shots that do not come off as planned (which happens even for very good golfers quite often!). Instead, choose a target that leaves considerable margin for error in the event that you do not pull of your shot as intended. This means playing to the fat part of greens, away from bunkers if you struggle out of the sand, and away from pins that would leave you short sided with a very difficult chip or pitch shot.

When you do get into trouble, your first priority should be to get out of trouble and back into play. Your thought process should be that hitting a bad shot into trouble may cost you one stroke, but you want to ensure that it does not cause you additional strokes by simply hitting your next shot back to safety. This means not trying to hit the miracle shot through that tiny window in the trees. Take your medicine, get the ball back into the fairway and go from there, even if it means bailing out sideways.

What happens all too frequently with higher handicap golfers is that they try to hit the spectacular miracle recovery shot and end up deeper in trouble and compounding their errors. In these situations you need to focus on minimizing the damage.

If you want to develop the ability to break 80 and shoot consistently in the 70s, it is essential that you adopt the strategy guidelines above and improve your on-course decision making. As you do, I believe you will be pleasantly surprised at the number of strokes you can save simply by thinking your way more intelligently around the golf course.

The Break 80 Mindset

Gaining the ability to consistently break 80 requires a different kind of mental approach than that of struggling golfers. Some experts claim that golf is as much as 90% mental. I personally don't believe the figure is quite that high. After all, without an understanding of proper technique and without proper practice and preparation, and of course, without developing the short game skills that we have already determined are so essential to scoring, even the most positive-minded golfer will likely struggle. However, there is no doubt that a player's mindset has a very strong impact on how one ultimately plays. This is equally true when it comes to breaking 80. In order to gain the ability to break 80 on a consistent basis, you will need to develop what I call the Break 80 Mindset, which is the mental approach you will need to adopt in order to ultimately play to your true scoring potential.

Therefore, let's take a look at the keys to mastering the Break 80 Mindset.

Self-image

Establishing the Break 80 Mindset begins with remaking your self-image as a golfer. Struggling golfers tend to have a poor self-image of themselves as golfers. Many struggling high-handicap golfers love to make jokes about how bad they are and commiserate with one another about their poor play. Let's face it, playing terrible golf can be frustrating and sometimes even downright embarrassing, particularly for struggling golfers who are otherwise very successful in other areas of their lives.

However, such a negative self-image and self-talk can be very debilitating when it comes to actually performing to your potential on the golf course. Therefore, it is essential that you focus on your golf successes, no matter how small or few and far in between they may be, and develop the habit of giving yourself encouraging, positive self-talk rather than beating yourself up for your bad play. Build on a new self-image of yourself as an "improving golfer" rather than simply a "bad golfer" and you'll be taking an important first step in developing the Break 80 Mindset.

Likewise, please avoid characterizing yourself as a "terrible golfer" and habitually bemoaning your poor play with other golfers. Instead, start to visualize yourself playing better and succeeding more. Rather than saying "I played terrible" and recounting your numerous failures on the course following a round, focus instead on what you did well and what you are improving on. Your improved self-image as a golfer is a very important first step toward real and lasting improvement on the course and on the scorecard.

Be Process Oriented

The Break 80 Mindset requires that you become process oriented rather than results oriented. This means that during your round, instead of getting hung up on and upset at that last hole you just took a triple bogey on, or that terrible shot you just hit, which stays in your head for the rest of the round, you remain focused on the hole and the shot you now face: selecting an appropriate target, visualizing the shot you want to play, going through your set-up routine, and finally, executing the shot to the best of your ability.

It is certainly natural to get upset when you hit a poor shot. When that happens, allow yourself to feel and even vent your anger, but after you do, you must let it go and then move on.

Focus on Task at Hand

Related to being process rather than results oriented is developing the ability to focus on the task at hand. Because golf is such a slow-moving game, it can be very easy to get ahead of yourself (focused on the future) or to remain fixated on a shot or hole you just played (focused on the past). However, the reality is that we can affect neither the recent past nor the impending future, other than by what we do in the present moment. If we just hit a horrible smother hook off the tee and now find ourselves in the trees, we can do nothing to alter the result of our previous shot. All we can do is focus intently on getting out of jail and going from there. Therefore, in order to master the Break 80 Mindset you must learn to focus on the task at hand out on the golf course, while not allowing your mind to become distracted by thoughts of past and future shots.

Ability to Shake Off Bad Shots and Holes

Every golfer, from Charles Barkley to Tiger Woods and everyone in between, has bad shots and bad holes. One of the things that separates successful golfers from unsuccessful golfers is the ability to shake off those bad shots and holes without letting them get stuck in the mind and affect the rest of the round. In order to master the Break 80 Mindset, you must develop a selective memory whereby you draw on your successes and quickly forget your failures. You must quickly let go of your bad shots and instead draw upon your good shots in order to boost your confidence.

Stay in the Present

Successful golfers are those who are able to remain in the present moment, particularly while they are playing a shot. Golf allows for plenty of time in between most shots, and so there is ample time for the mind to wander. There is nothing wrong with "smelling the roses" in between shots and enjoying your walk or ride down the fairway. In fact, the time in between shots is a good opportunity to shake off any ill-effects of poor shots, regroup, disengage and relax, but once it's time to play your shot, it's time to forget about yesterday's happenings and tomorrow's plans and zero your focus in on the present moment. By the time you're ready to play your shot, your entire attention should be focused on the task at hand, which is to execute your shot. Look at it this way. Over the course of a four-hour round of golf, most of that time is spent in between shots. We only spend a few minutes of our entire round actually in the process of hitting our shots. Therefore, in order to master the Break 80 Mindset, it is imperative that you focus and bring yourself back to the present moment once it's time to hit your shot.

Focus on Desired Outcome

During their round of golf, successful golfers see the fairways, greens, and holes they are intending to hit. Unsuccessful golfers see the trees and lakes and bunkers and rough and slopes that threaten to eat their shots alive.

In order to master the Break 80 Mindset, you must learn to focus on where you want your ball to go, rather than where you do not want it to go. It has been said that the mind cannot distinguish between positive and negative, but rather, it simply processes the information it is offered without judgment of right or wrong. Therefore, the mental command "don't slice the ball into that bunker" is actually interpreted by your mind as "slice the ball right into that bunker," since slicing and bunkers is what you are focusing on and the mind doesn't easily distinguish between "do" and "don't."

Instead, learn to focus your intention precisely on where you do want your ball to go, and generate self-talk that instructs your mind exactly what you want to do, rather than what you do not want to do. Adopting the target-oriented approach to shot making discussed earlier in the book will go a long way toward training yourself to focus on where you want the ball to go, and eliminating the destructive habit struggling golfers have of focusing out of fear on where you do not want your ball to go. Mastering the Break 80 Mindset requires that you focus on desired outcomes, rather than undesired outcomes.

Develop and Follow Your Routine

Every successful golfer has a pre-shot routine, which they follow to the letter out of habit. The purpose of a pre-shot routine is to prepare you to hit your shot by relying on a consistent set of pre-determined actions designed to put you in a state of readiness to perform the task at hand.

Every golfer's pre-shot routine is unique to that person, so you must develop your own routine of analyzing and seeing the shot you want to play, selecting a club, aligning your body, setting up properly, and initiating your actual swing.

It's interesting to note that when under intense pressure, even the best golfers in the world occasionally get out of their normal routine. When coming down the last hole with a chance to win a tournament, many golfers start to speed up, while others become overly deliberate. The best course of action is always to stick to your routine.

Of course, many struggling golfers do not even have an established pre-shot routine, but if you do not, begin today to establish your own. Your routine can certainly evolve over time, but begin by figuring out what you need to do in order to get comfortable and set up to hit each shot, and then go through that process on each and every shot you hit, in play and in practice. You'll find that this adherence to your routine will help put you in position to play each shot to the best of your ability.

Commit to Your Shot

Successful golfers tend to be committed to the shot they have chosen to play, whereas unsuccessful golfers tend to stand over their shot with their heads swimming in doubts and fears. Once you have decided on the shot you want to play, commit to that shot and do not second guess yourself. The shot may or may not come off as planned, but the likelihood of your shot being successful will be much greater if you stay committed to it than it will if you second guess yourself right before you pull the trigger.

Tolerate Your Mistakes

It is very rare to play a mistake-free round of golf. In fact, it is often said that golf is more about "managing your misses" than it is hitting perfect shots. The reality is that even the best players in the world miss many shots each round.

When you do hit a bad shot, in order to master the Break 80 Mindset you must quickly forgive your transgressions and allow for the fact that you are going to make your share of mistakes during your round.

One way to help you tolerate your mistakes is to establish your own personal par that reflects a realistic scoring goal based on your current ability, rather than the unreasonable par on the scorecard. For instance, even the goal of breaking 80 and shooting 79 on a par-72 course allows for seven one-stroke mistakes per round ($72 + 7 = 79$), which allows for a one-shot mistake on nearly half of the holes. If your goal is to break 90, this allows for only one less than a one-shot mistake on every hole ($72 + 17 = 89$)!

This type of perspective helps you to not panic when you do hit a poor shot, while enabling you to still remain focused on the task of shooting the lowest score you can on that particular hole.

Stay Patient

Most of the keys to the Break 80 Mindset that we have discussed so far boil down to one word: patience. When it comes to playing your best golf, the saying patience is a virtue has never been truer. Patience is essential both during each individual round of golf, and over the course of your golfing lifetime as you work to improve. While on the course, it is vital that you remain patient throughout the course of your round.

Manage Your Emotions

Golf is not a game that lends itself to extreme highs and lows of emotion. An emotional high following a great shot or hole can be just as adversely affect your next shot as an emotional low following a terrible shot or hole.

Therefore, the Break 80 Mindset requires that you constantly strive to keep an "even keel" while on the course, tempering your emotions so that you do not get overly excited when something good happens, nor overly upset when bad things occur.

Temper Your Expectations

Managing emotions is made easier by managing expectations. There is an inverse relationship between unfulfilled expectation and disappointment. That is, the greater your expectations, the more you are setting yourself up for disappointment when you do not reach them.

One way to manage expectations is to make sure that they are reasonable. One way to do this that we have already discussed is to establish a personal par that you can reasonably play to, rather than attempt to play to the unreasonable par on the golf course.

Another key to managing expectations about shooting a particular score is to realize that although we often characterize ourselves as being a golfer that shoots 95, 85, 125, or whatever the case may be, in reality, we seldom shoot our best score or even our median score every round. Rather, we tend to shoot scores on average within a particular range. So for instance, if you describe yourself as someone who shoots 85, in actuality, you probably shoot scores on average ranging from, say, 82 to 88. That is, your best scores at your current level can be a bit better than 85, while your worst scores are a few strokes higher. Any scores significantly higher or lower than these, at least until you improve an aspect of your game that impacts your ability to score (hint: short game!), can be considered outliers.

Framing your average range of scores in this way can help to temper expectations, because even when you shoot a score a few strokes worse than what you consider average, you can realize that the score you just shot was simply at the upper end of your scoring range. For example, if you characterize yourself as an 85 shooter and card an 82 for the day, you'll know that you've simply reached the bottom end of your scoring range. Similarly, if you have a terrible day at the course and end up with a

94, you can at least take comfort in the fact that your performance was an anomaly, so there is really no reason to panic about your game. Even tour pros occasionally shoot scores in the 80s.

Tempering expectations will help you focus and relax on the course, which in turn will enable you to play your best golf. Actually, my favorite state of mind in which to play golf is a state of no expectations at all. Even if I usually shoot about 78 and have an average scoring range of, say, 75 to 82, there is no guarantee that I am going to shoot a score within this range. On this particular day I could play much worse. Or I could play significantly better.

Instead, what I do is simply approach the first tee with the mindset of getting around the course in as few strokes possible, whatever the eventual outcome. My best rounds of golf invariably come during days when I can get into this "expectation-free" state of mind. I also find it a freer and more enjoyable state of mind from which to play.

Break 80 Fitness

Even allowing for the "Lumpy" Tim Herrons and "the Walrus" Craig Stadlers of the golf world, today's professional golfers are true athletes. In order to compete against the best of the best, pro golfers need to maintain a fitness level that not only allows them to swing the club at prodigious speeds, but walk and play 18 holes 4-6 times per week (including practice rounds) and, perhaps most importantly, put in the many hours of practice required to play at a top level without their bodies breaking down.

When it comes to the fitness level you will need to break 80, first the good news: you do not need to maintain the fitness level of a world-class athlete, or even a tour pro. Chances are you don't walk and play 18 holes every single day or put in grueling practice sessions lasting several hours, and, hopefully after reading this book, you no longer beat mountains of golf balls day after day.

Now the not-so-good news: if you want to break 80 consistently, there is a minimum level of fitness you do need to maintain. If you're adverse to exercise, don't worry. You don't have to run or lift heavy weights or otherwise train intensively in order to become a consistent 70s shooter. But you do need to maintain a minimum level of fitness that will permit you to consistently practice to the extent you need to maintain a break-80 level of play without your body succumbing to injury, as well as a fitness level that will enable you to play your best golf and withstand the mental and physical rigors of an 18-hole test of golf. With that in mind, let's take a look at the elements of fitness you will need to develop and maintain in order to play your best golf all the time.

Break 80 Strength & Flexibility

While you certainly don't need to be a power lifter in order to break 80, even a very light resistance training program that develops your overall physical strength can go a long way toward not only giving you that extra distance and clubhead speed you need to give your game an edge, but also to help your body withstand the rigors of repetitive stress that is unavoidable from performing a swing motion over and over again both in play and in practice.

The golf swing is truly a whole-body motion. Ideally you want to develop strength in your legs and hip flexor muscles to provide your swing with a solid base, a strong upper torso and forearms to swing the club, and last but not least, powerful core muscles to drive the swing motion and generate sufficient clubhead speed.

If weight training is not your thing, consider Pilates or yoga as effective alternative to build those all-important golf core muscles.

If you aren't interested in getting into the gym or doing any sort of fitness program at all, consider training by using a training device such as the Orange Whip or a Swing Fan (my personal choice), two aids that will provide weight and resistance while you swing and help you build and maintain the muscles you need to play your best golf while avoiding injury.

Whatever method you choose to strengthen and maintain your golf muscles, here's a little piece of advice that will save you future trips to see your chiropractor:

The golf swing is an extremely one-sided motion. Therefore, in order to maintain your body's balance, it is essential that you counter constant swinging to the left (for right-handers) with swings or a comparable motion to the opposite side.

I do this by having a left-handed club lying around that I periodically pick up and swing several times a day. I also like swinging the Swing Fan left-handed. This helps to keep my body in balance and my strength equal on both sides, and avoid throwing my spine out of alignment.

Before practicing this contingency, I would often throw my body out of alignment due to excessive, unbalanced swing motions to my left side (with my right-handed swing). The inevitable result was lower back pain and many trips to my chiropractor's office. By prudently counter-balancing my motion, I'm now free of both back pain and expensive doctor bills.

Equally essential to strength training is stretching. In order to play your best golf and avoid injury, it is vital that you stretch and loosen up before, during and after your play and practice. Consider using a foam roller or stabilization ball to stretch out your back at home. However, don't limit your stretching to just the times when you play golf. Make stretching a habit that you do on a daily basis without fail. A yoga-based stretching program is also great for increasing not only strength but flexibility as well. You don't need to spend tons of time stretching. Even as little as 5-10 minutes a day will do wonders for your flexibility, not to mention your ability to break 80.

Break 80 Endurance

Performing well at any sport requires a level of endurance specific to that sport. For example, top sprinters and marathon runners are both world-class athletes, but the type of endurance required for each sport is completely different. Such is the case with golf.

You might not think that endurance is an important factor when it comes to golf, but I'd like you to reconsider that notion. During an average round of golf, you typically walk as many as five miles over uneven terrain while stopping to swing a club every once in a while addition to shouldering or pushing along a heavy bag of clubs (if you walk).

Even if you ride a cart while you play, in order to break 80 consistently you still need to be just as engaged on the last hole as you were on the first, and whether you walk or ride, an 18-hole round of golf that lasts 4-5 hours can be physically as well as mentally draining.

When it comes to golf endurance, golf is definitely more of a marathon than it is a sprint. You want to be able to pace yourself over the course of 18 holes, and feel that you are still walking on fresh legs by the time you approach the home stretch of holes.

Likewise, sometimes it isn't the body that becomes exhausted at the end of a round but rather, the mind. Playing break-80 golf requires that you concentrate and stay engaged throughout the entire round, and this level of concentration can leave you drained. Furthermore, if you become physically tired midway through your round, this will likely affect your concentration and in turn, your ability to play your best golf.

Therefore, in order to build up your golf endurance, you need to not only build up your capacity to play 18 holes without physically tiring, but also your capacity to concentrate mentally over the course of an entire round.

To this end, consider incorporating a program of walking, jogging, or cycling as exercises away from the golf course to build up your golfing sea legs along with the physical and mental endurance you need to stay engaged over an 18-hole round.

Break 80 Nutrition

What you eat (and drink) will definitely impact your golf performance. While a healthy, balanced diet is important for maintaining your body's overall health, not to mention your ability to play your best golf, for now let's simply focus on how what we eat during a round of golf can affect our performance.

For many golfers, drinking and golf go hand in hand. Now as far as I'm concerned, there's nothing wrong with enjoying a few cold ones with friends during a recreational round of golf, but when it comes to playing for the purpose of maximizing your performance and shooting low scores, you're better off shelving your drinks until the 19th hole.

What you eat during a round can also impact your performance. High-calorie, high-sugar foods and drinks like hot dogs, candy bars and sodas that are commonly available at the course can cause you to get overly full and become sluggish, or even worse, cause your blood sugar levels to spike and then crash, leaving you feeling fatigued and unable to concentrate.

Therefore, in order to avoid sluggishness and "crashing" that can kill your concentration, not to mention your scorecard, opt instead for water as your go-to beverage during your round, and as mid-round snacks, consider lighter, healthier options like apples and bananas, almonds, peanut-butter sandwiches, or a low-sugar energy bar.

My own go-to in-round meal is a banana midway through the front 9, a peanut-butter bagel at the turn, and an energy bar later in the round if I need an additional boost.

Practice Break 80 Nutrition by staying fueled and hydrated during your round with energy-rich foods and plenty of water, and save the rich tasty treats and alcoholic refreshments and sodas for after the round, and you'll be well on your way to maximizing your performance and becoming a consistent 70s shooter.

Break 80 Preparation & Performance

In addition to what you do on an ongoing basis to maintain Break 80 Fitness, how you prepare for each individual round can greatly impact your performance on any given day.

Your Break 80 Preparation should begin well before your actual round does. Even before you leave the house, make sure to eat a healthy meal and pack foods, based on above the Break 80 Nutrition guidelines, which will help you stay fueled during your round. Stretch and loosen up at home so your body isn't tight when you arrive at the course. In addition to stretching for about 10 minutes or so, I also like take a couple dozen golf swings in my living room or backyard before I leave the house to help loosen up my body.

Use the drive over to the course to visualize your upcoming round and to get yourself into the Break 80 Mindset. Make an effort to get yourself in the right frame of mind to play your best golf.

Plan to arrive at the course sufficiently early to warm up a bit and not feel rushed. I personally don't like to hit a lot of balls before I play. I have found that if I hit balls before a round, when my ball striking is even just a bit off this can affect my confidence, so I usually opt to just trust that the work I've done on my game will get the job done. If I hit balls at all, I'll usually hit just a few wedges to find my rhythm, and then I'll hit a couple drivers to get a feel for my ball-flight tendencies for that day.

Whether or not you choose to hit balls prior to your round, make sure you spend a few minutes on the practice green before you play. Here's a 5-minute putting warm-up that I use when pressed for time to ensure that I'm ready to putt my best on the course.

-Take 2 balls and putt around a hole with some break from about 1.5 to 2 feet out. The goal here is simply to get a feel for how the ball is going to break near the hole while building up your confidence for the day by stroking putt after putt into the hole. If you happen to miss one of these, just pull it back and repeat until you make. Putt around the circle so you can see how the ball is rolling near the hole from each angle.

-After completing the above drill one time, now hit both balls across the entire length of all four sides of the practice green. Here, you want to get a general feel for the overall speed of the green.

-If you still have time, now just pick a few random holes to putt to, again to hone in on your distance feel. Choose holes of varying slopes and breaks to get a further feel for how the greens are rolling. Be sure to hit some downhill putts so that you can properly negotiate those slippery putts that can easily get away from you on the course.

-Finally, find a slightly uphill putt about 10-15 feet away and stroke a few putts toward the hole, emphasizing getting the ball to the hole. The goal here is simply to reaffirm a positive stroke to take with you to the course.

This little routine will help you maximize your putting performance that is so essential to shooting your best possible score. If you have any remaining time, hit a few chips to further get a feel for how the ball is landing and rolling on the green.

The above is my own approach to preparation before a round when pressed for time. The more time I do have, the more of it I spend warming up on the putting and chipping greens in order to hone my short game skills for that day. Feel free to experiment and find your own routine that enables you to be as prepared as possible to play your best golf.

Summary:
Putting it All Together

Let's now summarize the key points we have learned so far in the Little Book of Breaking 80.

The Problem with Conventional Golf Instruction

✓ Golf instruction, done correctly under the guidance of a capable instructor, is the surest path to improvement

✓ It is essential to find an instructor who fits your learning style

✓ While there are many excellent instructors, there are also many not-so-great instructors. Be sure to do your homework

✓ Find an instructor who will help you develop your entire game, not just your golf swing

✓ If you receive instruction, understand that learning and improvement is a process. Therefore, a single lesson, or even two or three, is not likely to help much, and may even leave you worse off than before

✓ Golf lessons require a significant investment of money, although significant improvement in golf will always require an investment, as some combination of time, energy, and money. Therefore, weigh the pros and cons and make a smart investment decision

Golf Information Overload

- ✓ There is a massive amount of golf information available to all golfers through such media as golf magazines, the Golf Channel, and the Internet

- ✓ Even fundamentally sound, logical, excellent advice may not apply to your specific needs

- ✓ When watching and learning from swing videos, incorporate the common fundamentals shared by all pros, but be careful about mimicking the unique style of any one golfer, as this may also leave you worse off than before

- ✓ Internet golf forums are full of conflicting, and sometimes not well-informed opinions, which can influence your golf game for the worse

- ✓ The Golf Channel is full of instructional segments, again, many of which may sound useful but may or may not be useful for you

- ✓ Most golf information will only overload your brain and confuse you, rather than help you

- ✓ The biggest enemy of golf improvement is information overload

- ✓ Therefore, when it comes to golf, it is essential to be very prudent about filtering out the useful from the harmful

Training Aids

- ✓ Some training aids are useful; some not so useful

- ✓ When using a training aid, use for its true function and ignore the promised results promoted by the aids, which are mostly hype

- ✓ Most aids are swing-focused, and while they may help you improve your swing, they do not address the scoring aspect of the game (short game). Therefore, the hype promoted by such aids (drop 7 shots in 90 days, etc.) is mostly bogus

- ✓ There are no magic pills in golf, and there is no one training aid that will magically transform you from a hacker into a scratch golfer

Instruction Books & Videos

✓ There is a wealth of instruction books and videos by the best teachers and players in the game

✓ While the instruction provided through these media may be very sound, there is no guarantee that it is precisely what you need for your game

✓ It can be difficult to successfully assimilate even the soundest instruction from books and videos into your own game

Equipment & Technology

✓ Even the incredible advances in equipment technology have not resulted in significant scoring improvement for golfers overall

✓ In order to play your best golf it is important to be properly fitted for equipment that is right for you

✓ While playing clubs that suit you most certainly can help you play and score better, avoid the temptation to believe that there are magic clubs out there that will transform your game. You still have to swing and pitch and chip and putt and think your way to good golf. Find the clubs that work best for you and stick with them, until you have a legitimate reason to change

How We Approach the Game of Golf

✓ Within the game of golf, there are two games that most golfers play: golf swing, and the actual game of golf

✓ Most struggling golfers are overly focused on the game of golf swing, to the detriment of playing the actual game of golf

✓ Many golfers have, or believe they have, a high theoretical "knowledge" of the golf swing and game of golf as a whole, but when it comes to golf, there is a vast difference between knowing what you think you know and being able to perform what you know

✓ Therefore, what you know about the game is less important than what you can do with what you know, or even what you can do without knowing how you do it!

How We Practice Golf

✓ Golf practice involves repetition, and therefore the formation of habits, whether good habits or bad habits

✓ Repetitive swing practice on the driving range without proper guidance or purpose results in the formation of a habitual swing motion which, once ingrained, can be very difficult to change

✓ Therefore, when it comes to golf, practice makes permanent, not perfect. Only perfect, precise practice results in perfect, precise results

✓ For most golfers, golf practice is overly swing- or full-shot focused

✓ Practice for most golfers involves beating balls on the range with no real purpose, and often, not even a defined target

✓ Putting practice for most golfers involves mindlessly slapping balls at holes for a few minutes, without any real structure or purpose to the practice session

✓ Few golfers seldom if ever practice their short games, and even fewer do so in a meaningful manner

✓ Despite the fact that as many as two-thirds of all shots in a round of golf are performed with less than a full swing, for most golfers, 90% or more of their practice is focused on the full swing

✓ Excessive ball beating on the range can lead to repetitive stress injuries. Therefore, when it comes to golf practice, quality most definitely trumps quantity

✓ Based on the 80-20 Rule, 80% of your scoring improvement comes from 20% of your effort. When it comes to golf, most of this 80% improvement from 20% of the effort can be found in the short game

The True Keys to Scoring

✓ When it comes to scoring in golf, the greatest impact on your score revolves around the short game

✓ Ball striking is of course an important part of golf. However, keep in mind that:

✓ As many as two-thirds of all shots in a round of golf are played from 100 yards and in with less than a full swing

✓ As many as fully one-half of all shots in a round of golf are played from 20 yards in

✓ As many as one-third of all shots in a round of golf are putts

✓ The closer the shot is to the hole, the greater negative impact not fulfilling the function of that shot has on your score

✓ Therefore, the clear path to better scoring is through improvement of the short game

Target-focused Golf

✓ At its essence, golf is a game of hitting targets

✓ The target for any given shot contracts and expands relative to the distance from the hole and difficulty of the shot

✓ Targets can also shift to or away from the hole or even the fairway and green based on the hazards that lurk nearby, such as trees, lakes, creeks, bunkers, and short sides of the green

✓ One should therefore select targets reasonable and appropriate for the shot at hand in combination with one's current skill level

✓ The smallest target, the hole, appropriate for short putts to medium-length putts, offers only a few centimeters of margin for error

✓ The largest target, the fairway and even the rough off of a drive, can offer as wide a target as 50 yards or more

✓ When it comes to target-focused golf, your shot does not have to be perfect; just good enough to fulfill the function of that particular shot

✓ Provided you hit the target appropriate for the shot at hand, you have fulfilled the function for that particular shot, even if your ball contact or ball flight was less than perfect

Shot-focused Golf

✓ Golf is also best played as shot-focused, rather than swing focused

✓ Swing-focused golf involves focusing on the nuances of the golf swing, to the distraction of focus on the actual desired outcome for the shot

✓ Shot-focused golf involves focusing on the specific type of shot (shape, trajectory, etc.) in order to hit your chosen target

✓ All accomplished golfers are shot-focused, rather than swing-focused golfers, particularly while playing a round of golf

The True Keys to Golf Improvement

✓ Swing mastery is elusive

✓ Many golfers spend decades on the range in the futile pursuit of swing mastery

✓ It is easier to become proficient at shots that are closer to the hole and require simpler motions

✓ Becoming proficient at shots closer to the hole will result in the greatest immediate scoring improvement

✓ Mastery of shorter shots establishes a foundation for subsequent mastery of longer shots

✓ Shorter shots are relatively easy to become highly proficient at compared to full shots; therefore, developing your skills using the "learn golf from the hole backwards'" approach will also enable you to experience more immediate success and provide you with a foundation of confidence in your growing shot making arsenal

Course Management

✓ Inexperienced golfers tend to lose many shots per round owed to nothing other than poor decision making

✓ It is possible to save strokes and score better simply by making better decisions on the course

✓ For most golfers, a conservative approach is the best approach

✓ Play to your basic shot shape

✓ Off the tee, play to the open side of the fairway and away from hazards

✓ Consider hitting a 3-wood or hybrid or iron off the tee if hazards lurk in your driver landing area

✓ Play to the fat part of the green and away from hazards

✓ Play your approach shots away from a tucked pin in order to avoid "short-siding" yourself

✓ Try to keep the ball below the hole

✓ If you get into trouble, your first priority is to get out of trouble, even if it means pitching back into the fairway or bailing out to the middle of the green

✓ Always think ahead while on the tee of the ideal angle you would like to approach your next shot from, and plan your shot accordingly while taking into account the hazards that lurk nearby

The Break 80 Mindset

✓ The ability to consistently break 80 requires the right kind of mental approach, or Break 80 Mindset

✓ The Break 80 Mindset is process rather than result oriented

✓ The Break 80 Mindset is focused on the task at hand in the present moment

✓ The Break 80 Mindset has the ability to quickly shake off bad shots and holes

✓ The Break 80 Mindset focuses on desired outcomes rather than undesired outcomes

✓ The Break 80 Mindset is committed to the chosen shot

✓ The Break 80 Mindset is patient and tolerant of mistakes

✓ The Break 80 Mindset is deft at tempering expectations and emotional highs and low

Break 80 Fitness

✓ Breaking 80 requires a reasonable level of fitness

✓ Consider some program or routine of strength training and stretching to develop your golfing muscles and endurance

✓ What you eat and drink during a round can affect the quality of your golf; therefore, stay hydrated with plenty of water and eat light, nutrition-packed snacks while you play to help keep you alert, engaged and energized

✓ Preparing properly prior to your round will help get you ready to play your best; therefore, develop a routine that helps you be ready once you get to the first tee

Your Break 80
Improvement Plan

Based on what you now know about what it takes to break 80 consistently, you now have in your possession the foundation of knowledge you need in order to put together an improvement plan that will virtually assure that you eventually gain the ability to break 80, provided you faithfully follow the principles outlined in this book.

Each golfer is unique in terms of natural talent, experience, current skill level, strengths and weaknesses, availability of facilities and resources, financial means, and practice time. Therefore, it is impossible to predict how long it will take to get from where you currently are in your game to the ability to break 80 on a consistent basis.

What I can say with relative certainty is that if you faithfully follow the principles outlined in this book, you will improve and your scores will begin to drop, in a linear, rather than haphazard progression. Beginning golfers and high handicappers should experience the biggest and quickest leaps in scoring improvement, since by following the principles of this book they will be most directly addressing the very issues that cause such players to lose the most shots. Even high handicappers and beginning golfers with significant ball striking issues will benefit from applying the Truth Keys to Breaking 80, because the surest path for these golfers to ball striking proficiency is actually to first establish a foundation of successful learning with shorter, easier shots (putts, chips, pitches, wedges, etc.) before moving on to the longer and more difficult-to-hit clubs.

Formulating Your Scoring Improvement Plan

The closer one gets to par golf, the more difficult it becomes to save those last few strokes over par. This makes sense when you consider that the closer one is to par, the fewer mistakes one is making on the course to begin with, and so there are fewer strokes available to save.

For most mid-handicap golfers, the majority of shots lost to par can be traced to weaknesses in the short game. Most mid-handicappers have at least a reasonable level of ball-striking proficiency. Minimally, such golfers are usually able to make consistently solid contact and advance the ball in the general direction of their target.

Although improvement in ball striking proficiency is always desirable, the level of ball striking described above is really all that is required to begin breaking 80 provided one has a well-developed short game and a strategic playing approach through sound course management.

With these observations in mind, following is my recommended approach to designing the most effective improvement plan for you:

- ✓ Make a commitment to developing those aspects of the game that will most impact your ability to score
- ✓ Devote the majority of your golf practice time to those aspects of the game that will most impact your ability to score
- ✓ Adopt the "learn golf backwards" approach as your long-term improvement plan
- ✓ The closer your shot is to the hole, the greater the impact on your score
- ✓ Short putts of about 10 feet and in represents your True Scoring Range—the range from which you can reasonably expect to actually hole out a high percentage of shots. Therefore, place

particular emphasis on improving your proficiency at holing short putts, as nothing will make as immediate and lasting difference in your ability to score

✓ Be sure to give ample attention to developing your short game around the green, and improving your ability to hit shot within the True Scoring Range

✓ When practicing, particularly full shots requiring full swings, always keep in mind the truism that when it comes to golf practice, "practice makes permanent; only perfect practice makes perfect"

✓ Hit fewer balls more deliberately, and always emphasize quality over quantity

✓ Spend more time working on and reviewing your grip, stance, and alignment and less time robotically beating balls on the range

✓ Always have a target in mind when you practice

✓ Work on improving your on-course decision making

✓ Work on improving your mindset

Sample Break 80 Improvement Plan

So how does one go about actually implementing an effective Break 80 improvement plan?

Following is a sample outline of a self-directed golf improvement curriculum that you can follow in order to develop your game with an emphasis on maximizing scoring improvement while building a foundation for better ball striking proficiency through improved proficiency with less than full swing shots.

Bear in mind that this is only one example of how you might implement the principles learned in this book, and that you should adjust performance benchmarks for each shot type based on your own current level of play.

Putting

Short Putting

Basic: practice putting in a circle around the hole from 12, 3, 6, and 9 o'clock and the four in-between positions. Hole out from each position for the following distances: 3 feet, 4 feet, 5 feet, and 6 feet. If you miss, simply repeat until you make and then move on to the next position.

Intermediate: perform same drill as above, but if you miss from a position, move back to the previous position and repeat before moving on and completing each putt from each distance.

Advanced: perform same drill as above, but if you miss from a position, move back to the first position for each distance until you make all of the putts from each distance without missing.

Medium-length Putting

Basic: from relatively flat putt, roll 5 balls within two-feet of hole for following distances: 10 feet, 15 feet, 20 feet, and 25 feet

Intermediate: perform same drill as above, but introduce various slopes and breaks

Advanced: perform same drill as above, but putts must all finish past the hole and on the high side of the hole

Lag Putting

Basic: from relatively flat putt, roll 5 balls within 4 feet of the hole from following distances: 30 feet, 40 feet, and 50 feet; hole out all balls with no 3 putts

Intermediate: perform same drill as above, but introduce various slopes and breaks.

Advanced: perform same drill as above, but all balls must finish no more than 3 feet from the hole

Chipping

Basic: hit 5/10 chips (little or no break or slope) with 1 yard of carry • from good lie to within 4-foot circle 20-30 feet away; misses no farther than 6 feet away

Intermediate: same as above, but now hit 7/10 within target circle

Advanced: same as above, but now hit 8/10 within target circle

(Variations: introduce various slopes, breaks and lies. Increase distance and required carry. Experiment with different clubs to find which clubs produce best results)

Pitching

Basic: 10-yard pitch: with a lofted club (SW or LW) from a good lie requiring about 1/3 carry and 2/3 roll). 5/10 within 6 feet; misses no farther than 10 feet away

20-yard pitch: with a lofted club (SW or LW) from a good lie requiring about 1/3 carry and 2/3 ½ roll). 5/10 within 8 feet; misses no farther than 12 feet away

30-yard pitch: with a lofted club (SW or LW) from a good lie requiring about 1/3 carry and 2/3 roll). 5/10 within 10 feet; misses no farther than 15 feet away

Intermediate: same as above, but now hit 7/10 within target circle

Advanced: same as above, but now hit 8/10 within target circle

(Variations: introduce various slopes, breaks and lies. Increase distance and required carry (1/2 carry and 1/2 roll; 2/3 carry and 1/3 roll, etc.). Experiment with different clubs to find which clubs produce best results)

Bunker Shots

Basic: hit 10/10 from 10-30 feet from good lie onto green

Intermediate: same as above, but now hit 5/10 from 10-30 feet within 15 feet of hole; misses on green

Advanced: same as above, but now hit 7/10 from 15-30 feet within 10 feet of hole; misses no farther than 15 feet away

(Variations: introduce various lies in sand various distances and carries. Reduce target size even further)

This sample improvement plan only covers a distance from the hole up to about 30 yards. Let me make a bold prediction. If you work on nothing else over the next year than attaining the proficiencies described above, it is a near certainty that you will either begin breaking 80, or be extremely close to doing so. At the very least, if you are a very high handicap golfer, you will experience a massive improvement in your ability to score.

What remains is to continue to refine your ball striking through intelligent and deliberate, rather than voluminous, practice, to continue improving your on-course strategy, so as to maximize the shots you save simply through better decision making, and to continue developing your Break 80 Mindset and Break 80 Fitness so that you're always in the right frame of body, mind and spirit to play your best golf.

Conclusion

The approach outlined in this book is the exact approach that enables me, after decades of confusion and inconsistency, to now break 80 on a regular basis. Just as importantly, it is the approach I now use to continue improving in a linear, rather than haphazard manner.

Now that you too have in hand the True Keys to Breaking 80, you can no longer claim ignorance as your excuse for a golfing performance that does not meet your expectations. Like Neo in the movie The Matrix, you now have but two simple choices:

The Blue Pill

If you take the Blue Pill, you may simply return to the conventional approach to golf which, for 98% of all golfers, simply does not work. Forget everything you read here and return to your regularly scheduled programming, doing what everyone else is doing, and getting similar results. Before you do so, however, please recall one final time the famous words of Albert Einstein:

> *"Insanity is doing the same thing over and over and expecting different results"*

The Red Pill

If you take the Red Pill, you will fully embrace the True Keys to Breaking 80, and begin to act on what you now know to be true. If you follow this path, do so as you recall the words of the famous poet Robert Frost:

"Two roads diverged in a wood, and I, I took the one less traveled by, and that has made all the difference"

I certainly hope that you join me in taking the Red Pill, embracing the True Keys to Breaking 80, and traveling on this journey down the Road Less Traveled of real and lasting golf improvement and scoring at a level that is beyond the reach of the majority of golfers who either have not yet grasped the True Keys to Breaking 80, or who simply choose to remain blissfully ignorant.

I thoroughly enjoyed writing this Little Book of Breaking 80 and sincerely hope that it will help you become the golfer you have always wanted to be. In closing, let me just remind you that golf, like life, is a journey rather than a destination. So in the words of the great Walter Hagen, when it comes to your golf game (and life):

"Don't hurry. Don't worry. You're only here for a short visit. So don't forget to stop and smell the roses"

If you enjoyed this book and found it helpful, please take a moment to provide your feedback with a positive review on Amazon.com.

For updates, articles, and more stroke-saving Break 80 instruction, please take a moment to "like" The Little Book of Breaking 80 Facebook page:

https://www.facebook.com/littlebookbreaking80

Thank you again for reading The Little Book of Breaking 80. I sincerely wish you the best of luck and improvement with your golf game!

Appendix 1:
Pro Shot-Making Averages

In order to help you establish your own shot-making benchmarks for each shot type, I have provided a table of performance averages of the PGA Tour pros. In compiling this table, I researched the Shotlink Stats on the pgatour.com website, using the 2012 stats. I provided three different stats for each shot type: average (the 90th ranked player, roughly the middle of the pack), best, and worst.

Naturally you cannot reasonably expect to perform at the same level as a Tour Pro. However, these benchmarks give you an idea of what type of performance is possible for each shot type. Refer to these performance measures, and then adjust them to your own reasonable level while working to get increasingly closer to the level of a tour pro. See if you can get closer and closer to the pro performance levels, particularly from the shots on and around the green.

Putting (% holed from each distance)

Distance:	Avg.	Best	Worst
3 feet:	99.28%	100%	98.02%
4 feet:	91.42%	99.06%	75.81%
5 feet:	81.19%	95.89%	56.25%
6 feet:	68.83%	84.31%	54.72%
7 feet:	61.29%	77.42%	37.14%
8 feet:	53.06%	71.43%	22.22%
9 feet:	46.15%	73.33%	17.39%
10 feet:	41.67%	68.00%	19.05%
10-15 feet:	30.28%	40.83%	20.63%
15-20 feet:	18.24%	26.75%	9.68%
20-25 feet:	11.54%	26.79%	1.54%
25-30 feet:	0.82%	2.24%	0.0%

Notes:

From the closest distance, 3 feet, tour pros make virtually all of their putts. From the furthest distance range, 25-30 feet, pros rarely make a putt.

Putting (3-putt avoidance (% of 2-putts)

Distance:	Avg.	Best	Worst
5-10 feet:	99.6%	100%	97.2%
10-15 feet:	99.2%	100%	95.5%
15-20 feet:	98.4%	100%	92.5%
20-25 feet:	97.6%	100%	91.4%
25+ feet:	90.5%	95.5%	83.3%
8 feet:	53.06%	71.43%	22.22%
9 feet:	46.15%	73.33%	17.39%
10 feet:	41.67%	68.00%	19.05%
10-15 feet:	30.28%	40.83%	20.63%
15-20 feet:	18.24%	26.75%	9.68%
20-25 feet:	11.54%	26.79%	1.54%
25-30 feet:	0.82%	2.24%	0.0%

Notes:

From 25+ feet, the % of 3-putts becomes greater than the percentage of makes.

Chipping and Pitching

(Average proximity (in feet & inches) to the hole from following distances)

Distance:	Avg.	Best	Worst
Fringe:	3.1	2.0	4.7
~10 yards:	3.7	2.7	5.1
10-20 yards:	6.11	5.3	8.8
20-30 yards:	9.4	6.9	12.0
30+ yards:	12.8	8.0	18.0
Sand:	9.8	6.11	14.11

Notes:

From within 10 yards most pros hit the ball to within imminent hole-out range. Even from 10-20 yards, most pros hit the ball well within the True Scoring Range. From 30 yards and beyond, as well as from sand, even tour pros are more likely to take 3 shots to get into the hole than 2.

Scrambling Proficiency

(% up-and-down conversions from the following distances)

Distance:	Avg.	Best	Worst
Fringe:	88.89%	100%	71.43%
~10 yards:	84.34%	97.62%	70.49%
10-20 yards:	63.35%	75.45%	45.24%
20-30 yards:	51.39%	66.15%	34.00%
30+ yards:	27.14%	41.86%	8.33%
Sand:	50.00%	70.59%	23.68%
All:	57.37%	64.34%	48.30%

Notes:

From within 10 yards, most pros get up and down virtually every time. From up to 30 yards, pros, on average, are able to get the ball up and down at least half the time. From all distances combined, almost all pros get the ball up and down at least half the time. From beyond 30 yards, pros are much more likely to take 3 strokes than 2 to get the ball in the hole.

Approach Shots

(Average distance to the hole (feet and inches)
from the following distance ranges (in yards))

Distance:	Avg.	Best	Worst
50-75:	15.5	6.11	27.2
75-100:	17.2	12.1	24.7
100-125:	19.11	16.0	25.5
125-150:	23.2	19.3	27.10
150-175:	27.8	22.8	34.4
175-200:	34.2	29.6	40.1
200-225:	40.9	34.0	54.11

Notes:

For most pros, even from 50-75 yards away, the average distance from the hole is well outside the True Scoring Range. From beyond 175 yards, the average distance to the hole is likely to yield more 3-putts than 1-putts.

Greens in Regulation

(% of greens in regulation from the following distance ranges (in yards))

Distance:	Avg.	Best	Worst
75-100:	80.56%	93.88%	64.29%
100-125:	76.14%	86.62%	62.50%
125-150:	71.07%	82.52%	54.84%
150-175:	63.78%	72.95%	49.64%
175-200:	54.07%	65.13%	42.80%
200+:	44.54%	62.50%	29.90%
All:	64.68%	70.34%	56.90%
Fairway:	75.64%	81.97%	67.97%
Non-fairway:	50.81%	60.73%	38.36%

Notes:

Pros on average only hit about 65% of all greens, and from rough and bunkers, only about 50% on average. From 175-200 yards, even tour pros have a difficult time hitting more than 50% of greens from those distances.

Driving

(% of fairways hit)

Distance:	Best	Worst
61.61%	72.97%	47.01%

Notes:

On average pros hit just over 61% of fairways, and many barely hit 50% of fairways.

CPSIA information can be obtained
at www.ICGtesting.com
Printed in the USA
BVOW09s1940160817
492240BV00013B/163/P